A Poetry Chronicle

A Poetry Chronicle

Essays and Reviews
by
IAN HAMILTON

FABER AND FABER
3 Queen Square London

First published in 1973
by Faber and Faber Limited
3 Queen Square London WC1
Printed in Great Britain by
Latimer Trend & Company Ltd Plymouth
All rights reserved

ISBN 0 571 10228 X
(Paper Covers)

ISBN 0 571 10175 5
(Hard Bound Edition)

Preface

I have been writing regular poetry reviews for just over ten years now, and this book is a selection of what seem to me my least ephemeral pieces. I have printed them more or less as they first appeared in periodicals, limiting revision to the adjustment of sloppy phrasings and resisting the temptation, stronger in some cases than in others, to amplify and extend. My hope is that the book, whatever is thought of its opinions, will serve some kind of documentary purpose; that, at worst, it will offer a reasonably detailed (though hardly all-inclusive) picture of what has been happening in poetry during the last decade.

I have been very fortunate with my editors and both Terry Kilmartin of the *Observer* and Arthur Crook of *The Times Literary Supplement* have been particularly kind and helpful over the years. My special gratitude, though, must be to Alan Ross of the *London Magazine*. He gave me my first regular reviewing job, allowed me a wholly undeserved amount of space and was tolerant of even the most callow of my indignations.

Contents

Songs Among the Ruins

If the contest between the 'cooked' and the 'raw' in American poetry no longer rages with the ferocity that enlivened the great Beat versus Brooks-and-Warren comedies of the 1950s, there has been no abandonment over the past five years of the main effort that lay behind those quarrels; the effort, that is, to define and demonstrate the American-ness of American poetry, to cut it loose from the more stifling of European cultural precedents, to renounce wit, learned ironies and the general tyranny of Guggenheim. For the Black Mountain poets this has involved an absorbed sophistication of the modernist theories of William Carlos Williams and the Objectivist group, an almost total preoccupation with technique and the oddities of native respiration. For less organized talents it has now and then meant something more profound.

In the best works of poets like Robert Lowell, John Berryman and Sylvia Plath one finds not just a cerebral attempt for the distinguishably United States idiom but an impassioned exploration of whatever chances the imagination still has of making sense of a civilization that is bent on self-destruction, that cruelly cannot fail to involve the poet in its manic processes but demands also that he survive as guardian of what is being killed; to these poets America is distinct from other societies in the sense that it is more efficiently dehumanizing, having abused its promise as it now prepares to abuse its power, and the best that they feel able to attempt is to oppose its abstracting pressures with the full weight of whatever in their own lives seems concretely worth saving. Sylvia Plath is dead, and the poetry of both Lowell and Berryman is rich with the despairing recognition that they will surely fail to transmute into valid wisdom the fragments of history which they both hoard and flee.

In *For the Union Dead* (1965) Lowell's extremes are his familiar ones, of paradise and purgatory; 'We know how the world will end', he writes, 'but where is paradise?' Those moments of nostalgic recall that so beautifully flare up in poems like 'Old Flame' or 'The Lesson' have only the power to hurt; it is in spite of love that we are 'wild spiders crying together' who are doomed to nuclear extinction, who must crack up or hit the bottle, or cling in desperation to the imagery that can merely measure our predicament. Jonathan Edwards' shadow falls as darkly over Lowell's most recent poems as it ever did on Lord Weary's Castle, and there are now no consoling Catholic rituals, nor even any family albums. The relaxed, digressive sadness of *Life Studies* is tightened up into a sustained, but never hysterical, alarm.

There is no other poet writing at the moment who can match the dense visual accuracy of Lowell's best work; his concentration is insistently upon 'the stabbing detail', his intense demand is always for 'the universal that belonged to this detail and nowhere else'—nothing is inertly factual, nothing is neurotically corrupted; there is fever, but no delirium. By an immensely subtle process of reverberation, his images seem to seek each other out, not to be wise so much as to be confirmed in tragedy, and they are interpenetrated in a structure tight enough to encompass their full range of connotation without any loss of urgency. In the title poem, for example, there is the minimum of actual comment; what seems at first a local scandal is intensified—without the reader really having noticed how—to reveal itself as a profound upheaval in the whole of nature, an 'earthquake', a dinosaur that eats into the heart of America, a nuclear explosion. What really impresses, though, is that even with this much evidently conscious shaping it still comes over as a deeply personal lament for those American images, both private and public, that have meant most to the poet and that are now braced for extinction. Lowell has fought hard to rid himself of Boston, but has returned to it time and again, probing nearer every time towards what he sees as the root of its, and America's, corruption, from the apocalyptic pulpitry of his early poems through the movingly ambivalent elegies of *Life Studies* (1959). In this new book it seems much less the private burden of a Mayflower aristocrat, and much more a richly emblematic means of giving voice to the sort of anguished perceptions about modern America that could only spring out of a deep involvement in what Boston can still, if feebly, point to as its failed historical mission.

In a much more quirkily disorganized way, a poem like John Berryman's *Homage to Mistress Bradstreet* (1959) makes a similar effort of disenchanted excavation, though his mission is much more explicitly that of the alienated artist re-creating the origins of the American effort to make poetry out of a hostile, repressive environment. Anne Bradstreet, a minor poet of the seventeenth-century Colonial School and often thought of as the first American poet, is imagined as having had her real talent thwarted by the rigid codes of New World puritanism; she is seen as 'hopeful and shamefast, chaste, laborious, odd', her life is hedged in, morosely zealous, allowing only intermittent, and then guilt-ridden, flights of creative fantasy. Her verse is 'bald abstract didactic', but not so the verse she addresses to the author of her *Homage*; this has all the wayward energy of Berryman's own style, its syntax dislocated almost beyond repair, its word-orders riotously deranged. Anne's situation, of course, serves as a means for Berryman to explore his own Americanness, and to focus his view of himself as an artist plagued by the demands of a world that has no valid role for him. Even in his most Audenesque moods, Berryman had never seemed at home as a responsible, symptomatizing public poet. Throughout his work there is a very specific sense of a victimized isolation from those millions whose 'happiness runs out like water' and whom the poet ought to be able to help.

In Berryman's most recent book, *77 Dream Songs* (1964), his alienation seems more fully acknowledged and extreme than ever before, and his style—teeming again with ampersands, accents, antiquated past-participles, zany inversions and so on—seems even more perverse. The songs themselves are spoken by Henry, who is presented variously as a scholar, a writer of mad books, an avid movie-fan, a spinner of sexual fantasies, a demented worshipper, a

clown; he is 'at odds wif de world and its god', and is the victim
perhaps just of his own 'ruin-prone mind'. Intermittently his voice
shades into, or cross-talks with, that of Mr. Bones, or of the poet
himself, and between them they meander into jokes, obituary, back-
chat, prayer, and reverie both comic and terrified; they touch on
politics, literature, psychoanalysis, racial prejudice, etc., but never in
any sustained, point-making fashion—the total gesture is one of
frenzied gesticulation against the God who has left things so messy,
absurd and hideously doomed. Demolishing the language may at
least pretend this kind of justification, that poetry ought not in a
maddened world to mimic sense and shapeliness but should aim instead at some sort of representative derangement, but there is more
than a little naughtiness involved, too, and this can get very boring.
Where Henry cracks, though, and is robbed even of the mad identi-
ties that his songs have now and then granted him, he finds that after
all he *is* gutted, ancient, dead-in-life; he is as negative and abstract as
the core of his poem, and his jokes have all been posthumous. This is
the book's most moving note, and it is worth waiting for:

> *There sat down, once, a thing on Henry's heart*
> *So heavy, if he had a hundred years*
> *& more, & weeping, sleepless, in all them time*
> *Henry could not make good.*
> *Starts again always in Henry's ears*
> *the little cough somewhere, an odour, a chime.*

There is a danger, of course, of this kind of dead perception being
regarded as the only valid consequence of pushing the modern
imagination to its proper extremes, and a number of respectable
theorists would argue that anything short of total breakdown is
trivial and narrowly self-defensive; that a derangement of the motive
and the power to reflect *within* what is being suffered is poetry's new
obligation. Too often it has been on these very treacherous grounds
that the achievement of Sylvia Plath's last poems has been hailed.
Like John Berryman, Sylvia Plath from the start sees the Imagination as a sanctuary, a retreat for the artist who finds herself adrift in

a hateful world—at its most perfect, the sanctuary is most death-like, and at its most turbulent, it is most deranging—madness and death are anyway seen as the likely outcome of its pursuit; what her best poems demonstrate, though, is that it is possible to suffer the full consequences of this perception and yet at the same time make the only kind of moral choice that we can now insist on from our poets —the choice of life against death, of the human rather than the brutal, of the reflecting imagination rather than the engulfing night-mare. This choice has of course got to be made in full possession of the facts, out of a full sensitivity, that is, to precisely those modern horrors that Sylvia Plath exposed herself to. To confuse the defeat of her life with the triumph of her art is to do her a cruel injustice.

Even in the elaborate, rhetorical poems of her first book, *The Colossus*, it is evident that she saw herself as already consigned to the bell jar that she writes of in her novel of that title. The bell jar links up with all the coffins, the morgues, the beehives, the wombs, the refrigerated babies, and so on, that swarm throughout her work— it seals her off from a world that she can still see, however distortedly, but it permits her that suspended, featureless anonymity that she always seems to be craving. How to escape from its imprisonment into the sort of fully expressive self-awareness that poetry needs, how to do this and yet still function as mother, housewife, villager, etc.—this becomes more and more the basis of her anguished vacilla-tion between a vision of death as something which will efface her silently and benevolently or as a transformation from which she will emerge as a kind of elemental queen, radiant, bountiful, angelic.

One of the most remarkable qualities of her work is that she is in-variably able to root this conflict in the solid details of her daily life, her domestic chores, her beekeeping and horse-riding; time and again she is plunged into complex nightmare through what seems at first a fairly homely trapdoor—as in 'Mary's Song', where the frying of the Sunday lamb is made to scorch across the whole of recent history and be seen finally as a holocaust. This is a tremendously difficult thing to have brought off and the myth-making gestures in her work do not always work as well as they do here—but it was impossible for her not to see herself as the volunteer arch-victim of all the torments of this century, not to offer up her least experience in service to this obligation.

When other people appear in Sylvia Plath's poems, they are usually seen as members of a 'pea-nut crunching crowd' who gloat over the spectacular agonies of the poet, and nearly all the men in her poems appear in black. In one way or another they are in direct descent from the loved and hated father who dominates all her work; he does so in a weird, obsessive fashion (she spoke of her Electra complex once, in a broadcast, but that does not really explain anything) and her imaginative pursuit is often fatalistically bound up with his posthumous control over her, his invitation that she come to him again, in death. In 'Sheep in Fog' she finds a metaphor that beautifully reconciles both the threats and promises of such an invitation:

> *My bones hold a stillness, the far*
> *Fields melt my heart.*
> *They threaten*
> *To let me through to a heaven*
> *Starless and fatherless, a dark water.*

There is something here, but far more subtly, of what she seems to be saying in her famous cry, 'Daddy, daddy, you bastard, I'm through.' Not only has she had enough, she has also finally *got through* to him—and in the only way possible, by the telephone lead that, cut off, hangs horribly, a root and then a worm; she gets through to Daddy but as always, though at last thankfully, no one can get through to her. This is often true of Sylvia Plath's own poetic voice, and there is much in her work that is impenetrably self-indulgent; her transitions are sometimes too fractionally or too arbitrarily achieved and she is over-ready to expose herself to the accidents—though now and then these are marvellous—of free-association. To group her with Robert Lowell, as some critics have, at the head of a supposed 'confessional' school of American poets is surely one of the more ludicrous of current pigeon-holings; there is

little in either poet's work of the flat, almost documentarily infor-
mative, kind of unburdening that one finds in, say, Anne Sexton—
who is often written up as one of their 'confessional' disciples. Miss
Sexton has clearly picked up a trick or two from the more prosy of
Lowell's *Life Studies*, and often seems to aim for the poignancy of
the absurdly literal. She is also prepared to let us have rather 'intimate' details of her personal life, and in particular of her stay in an
asylum. If these, or the kind of personal revelations that W. D.
Snodgrass makes in his *Heart's Needle*, are what is needed to make a
poet 'confessional', then either the term has only the most superficial usefulness or it is going to be difficult to find poets whom it
does not describe. Is Eliot 'confessional', for instance, or Philip
Larkin? The point is, perhaps, that unlike Larkin or Lowell, Miss
Sexton does very little with the facts; except in a handful of fierily
concentrated poems in her first book, *To Bedlam and Part Way
Back*, she merely hands them over.

To erect a slavish fidelity to data into a principle for modern poetry
is perhaps one academic way of bringing the 'subjectivists' of
American poetry in line with the 'objectivists' ('no feelings but in
facts' might be the general cry) but it surely has no more serious
function; certainly it would not satisfy the other well-publicized
'school' of American poets, those propagandists for the 'new
imagination' who write for Robert Bly's Sixties Press. These include
some of the most impressive new American talents; James Dickey,
Louis Simpson and James Wright are all associated in some way
with Bly's general effort for the 'period of surrealism' which
America has yet to experience, and—via Spain—the achievement of
a style which is common to both North and South America. Robert
Bly is unfortunately not the most eloquent of crusaders, and there
has been a good deal of mystification and apparent contradiction in
his various manifestos; the most useful of these is his introduction to
the collection of Sixties Press poetry, *The Lion's Tail and Eyes*, in
which he rejects the 'poetry of pictures' (his version of Pound's
imagisme) along with direct statement, realistic description, irony,

B

anecdote, any kind of rationalizing cleverness. The 'deep image' proceeds direct from the 'unconscious' and while it is being experienced has the power to transform not only the external world of objects and events but also our dead assumptions about the world.

Put like that, the theory might seem to leave little room for the sort of discriminating sensibility that appears in the best work of Wright and Simpson; in Wright's *The Branch Will Not Break*, for instance, there is a good deal of the wispily evocative dream-spinning that is the obvious danger of any literal practice of Bly's theories (indeed, Bly's own *Silence in the Snowy Fields* seems curiously artificial in its wide-eyed, loving swoons into the Minnesota landscape), but there is also a redeeming toughness and intelligence—this does not dull or narrow the poetry's imaginative effort but seeks to weigh its meaning, its power for good, its chances of survival, in terms of its total American environment. To propose this as the necessary task of the American poet is not—conditions being what they are— to grudge the kind of wistfulness that appears in Robert Bly's epigraph to the Sixties Press anthology. 'Poems written out of laziness and silence', he sighs; and he is surely not alone in wishing that such things were possible.

1965

The Waste Land

There can be few poems that have demanded and received as much exegetical piety as *The Waste Land*. It is the supreme puzzle poem and most of it has now been puzzled out. We have the allusions noted in the margins, we have flicked through *The Golden Bough* and *From Ritual to Romance* (comforted here by the information that Eliot's own copy has some uncut pages), we know—or think we know—what *shantih* means. So intimately has our experience of the poem been involved with the business of explication that it has become almost impossible for us to make the right kind of distinction between the words themselves, their actual resonance, and the scholarly murmurings that now encrust them. Lines tend to trigger off labyrinthine, half-remembered footnotes rather than evoke direct emotional responses. Or, to put it differently, and in spite of Eliot's own tag about poems communicating before they are understood, we have been encouraged to suspect that 'emotional responses' are somehow unreliable if they have not first been sieved through the meshes of our mugged-up learning.

Of course, Eliot wanted the poem to be difficult and no doubt conceived of its difficulty as an important aspect of its total meaning. There is the practical difficulty of the poem's wealth of cultural allusion and there is the deeper, but related difficulty of its general structure; a difficulty of detail and of plan. Dozens of attempts have been made to provide plausible solutions, to document the allusions, to guess at Eliot's structural intentions, and the assumption has invariably been that a poem which flourishes so many interesting signposts must know where it's going, that all the critic needs is to be more learned and ingenious in his interpretations than the next man. Eliot's knotty seriousness of aim has hardly been called in question— although when lines here and there have not fitted into the explicator's explication there have been nervous mumblings of discontent.

Explicator-in-chief and now the recognized guide to Eliot's aims is Grover Smith, author of *T. S. Eliot's Poetry and Plays: a study in sources and meaning* (1956) and, if only because thousands of students every year are likely to be poring over his interpretations, it might be worth glancing at a sample of his work. The bracing thing about Grover Smith is that he has so few doubts as to the absolute validity of his analyses. If Eliot hadn't written *The Waste Land*, Smith would surely have been able to invent—or at least paraphrase—it. For instance, he is able to tell us what we might not otherwise have been so sure of, that the opening lines of *The Waste Land* are spoken by Tiresias, and that in them, 'Blind and spiritually embittered, Tiresias wrestles with buried emotions unwittingly revived' (p. 72). There is, of course, nothing in the actual lines to tell us who is talking; it is simply that Smith has dutifully taken Eliot's gnomic note to heart and has determined to base a whole edifice of paraphrase upon it. Thus, since, 'What Tiresias *sees*, is the substance of the poem,' it is Tiresias who remembers

> another springtime, in his youth, when warm days of the resurrection season brought rain, the water of life, with sunlight, and he was beside the Starnbergersee near the city of Munich. A voice of a Lithuanian girl who recounted a childhood experience of terror, exhilaration, and freedom comes back to him. Against the double happiness of her memory and his, he must now set the present reality of the loveless, arid desert within him. He thinks of Ezekiel, the 'son of man' . . . (pp. 72–3).

In his anxiety to forge these neat mimetic links, and to erect a shapely incongruity between past pleasures and present grumbles, Grover Smith blithely ignores what ought, at any rate, to be considered as a *possibility*: that the memories are *not* those of the protagonist himself (whether or not he is Tiresias) but are being recounted to him by someone else, someone he disapproves of. The evidence suggests someone middle-aged, female, of cosmopolitan background, someone neurotically clinging to remembered frag-

ments of childhood experience, someone anxious to assert her
aristocratic origins ('the archduke's,/My cousin's'/: an over-eager
parenthesis), someone rather desperate and rather boring. One need
look no further than, say, 'Portrait of a Lady' or, indeed, the opening section of 'The Fire Sermon' to find an echo of the exhausted,
edgy intimacy of lines like

> *In the mountains, there you feel free.*
> *I read, much of the night, and go south in the winter.*

Far from setting a 'double happiness' against his present discontent,
it seems likely that the woman's recollections, their fevered, discon-
nected style, are being invoked by the protagonist in illustration of
'the loveless arid desert' he goes on to contemplate:

> *What are the roots that clutch, what branches grow*
> *Out of this stony rubbish?*

Grover Smith glides over these crucial lines, presumably because
they are in glaring contradiction of his chosen thesis. But one could
wrangle like this for hours. All in all, *The Waste Land* has been a
goldmine for explicatory critics and, while valuing many of the
nuggets they have dug up, we are still left with the problem of what,
as poetry, all the unravelled ingenuity adds up to. To what essential
poetic purpose are the various quotations, echoes, innuendoes that
keep forcing our attention back to other writers, other cultures? At
what level of seriousness is the anthropological backcloth deployed?
To what extent can the poem be said to justify the claims that have
been glibly made for it as an illuminating, massively inclusive, revelation of what modern life is really like? Are the ideas really trans-
muted into poetry or are they just ideas? And are they good ideas?
These might seem fairly primitive questions but they are nothing
like as simple-minded as four decades of academic tinkering have
encouraged us to think. Indeed, these are the only kinds of question
now worth asking.

The poem's most obvious peculiarity, that it is packed with lines,
or hints of lines, written by other poets, is now contentedly taken

for granted. We know where the borrowings came from and can easily persuade ourselves that they are valuably relevant. We know, too, that it was one of Eliot's profoundest feelings that, 'The people which ceases to care for its literary inheritance become barbaric.' Literature has a crucial civilizing function to perform and one of the ways in which it can sustain this function in a hostile age is simply to remind the present of the past, to insist that culture is continuous and that if people want a modern literature they can have it only at a price—the price, that is, of caring more about the literature they already have. But telling people what they should have read is not the same as showing people what they might have felt. It is not simply that Eliot drops more names, more scraps of cultivation, more bits and pieces of odd learning than the poem really manages to make serious use of—though this could well be argued. It is more that at the source of Eliot's confident allusiveness there seems to be a very personal despair which he is more interested in disguising than exploring.

At one level, the poem masquerades as Eliot's *ABC of Reading*, his comfortably pedagogic account of what our literary inheritance most valuably consists of. But his desire to educate doesn't get the sharp edge it needs from his despondent recognition that his audience is not only ignorant about culture but indifferent to it. It is true that Eliot is only prepared to go so far to meet his reader's ignorance and is as concerned to condemn indifference as to cure it, but condemnation is different—colder, duller—than complaint. Alongside the keen anthologizing there is a prim, aristocratic aloofness, a determination to keep up the barriers even as he pleads for their removal. Knowledge of some literary source is often a necessary condition of our grasping Eliot's point that such knowledge cannot generally be hoped for. Thus the poem is at once a display and a withholding of that possessed cultural wealth which, it is constantly implied, no one can afford to be without.

What one looks for in *The Waste Land* is something of Prufrock's wry self-knowledge. There is a hint of it in the notes, but not really in the poem itself. Prufrock is fastidious to the point of social paraly-

sis, and it is the sorry interplay between his dreams and his responsibilities that makes his love song moving. In *The Waste Land* there is
a similarly sorry interplay implied between poetry itself and its
likely audience (between, almost, an overvaluing and an under-
valuing of culture's powers) and there is something very Pru-
frockian in the situation of—shall we say?—a solemn, over-cultivated
New Englander whose cultural experience of Europe is far deeper,
he discovers, than that of most Europeans, a bookish sensitive adrift
among the philistines, cherishing intensities and insights which he is
convinced would cure a sickness whose chief symptom is indifference
to its most effective remedy. 'I am not Prince Hamlet, nor was
meant to be'; there is a similar despondent helplessness in the lines
from *Hamlet* which end 'The Game of Chess' but here one is not so
sure that Eliot is aware of it. Certainly one implication of 'goodnight, sweet ladies, goodnight, goodnight' is that if either May or
Lil were able to recognize the quotation, place it in context and
scrutinize its implications, they would be making a first step towards
some kind of spiritual recovery. We who do recognize it are
allowed, rather facilely, to feel superior to those who do not. The
essential difference between 'Prufrock' and *The Waste Land* is that
the earlier poem has a distinct human personality at the centre of it
whereas *The Waste Land* merely has a body of ideas and theories.
The personality we have to guess at.

There is a sense, certainly, in which May and Lil themselves might
be allowed to feel a twinge of lofty compassion for those who
habitually observe life through a haze of literature, those who have
read more than they are interested in experiencing. The judgements
of *The Waste Land* are the judgements of a supremely literary sensibility and one can detect an unacknowledged pathos in the ready
stock of futile, apt quotations, the lonely invocation of dead kindred
spirits. There is this whole aspect to *The Waste Land*, and the glum
pedantry of some of the explanatory notes might seem deliberately
to draw our attention to it. But had Eliot been as ready, in the poem
itself, to pass judgement on his own peculiar, crippling refinement
as he is to condemn other people's peculiar, crippling vulgarity, we

would have a different, more complex and affecting work than we are actually left with.

We might not, at any rate, have quite such a facile equation of cultural self-consciousness with spiritual prosperity. In 'Prufrock' Eliot captured a whole species of sophistication in the lines 'In the room the women come and go/Talking of Michelangelo'. The kind of dilettante cultivation, the smart highbrow chattering that is evoked here expresses lives every bit as desolate and pitiable as those of the lonely men in shirt-sleeves, leaning out of windows. Indeed, the lonely men seem, by contrast, rather worthy, contemplative creatures—had they been, say, quietly meditating on the work of Michelangelo they might even have come close to winning Eliot's approval. One of the troubles with *The Waste Land* is that its whole method tends to play into the hands of the chattering women rather than the lonely men, it tends to flatter those who know the cultural score and to despise those who don't.

It would be sheer simple-mindedness to pretend that being able to spot the allusions in *The Waste Land* guarantees anything about any-body. If one happens, though, to be an ill-read house-agent's clerk one will feel more sharply accused by 'The Fire Sermon' than if one is, say, an assistant professor of English literature. Whatever his sex life is like, the assistant professor will be on to that Goldsmith refer-ence in an instant and will therefore feel himself to be in comfortable conspiracy with the learned poet. Not only that, but when Eliot writes:

> *Burning burning burning burning*
> *O Lord Thou pluckest me out*
> *O Lord Thou pluckest*
>
> *burning*

and solemnly informs us that, 'The collocation of these two re-presentatives of eastern and western asceticism, as the culmination of this part of the poem, is not an accident,' the assistant professor might well be able to console himself that he is not the only well-read dabbler.

For Eliot, of course, a superb trinity of culture, sex and religion is humanity's most worthy goal and the sickness of modern civilization is that the three impulses operate in isolation. In a sense, though, Eliot's treatment of them maintains their separateness; the urged collaboration is mostly in the realm of theory. For example, although his distaste for casual sexuality is emotionally based on a conviction that sexuality is sacred, that it is in some way involved with, or endorsed by, religious feeling, his actual treatment of it in the poem is informed predominantly by revulsion. There is an almost gloating intransigence in his characterization of the squalidly unfeeling, the cheaply lustful possibilities of human conduct. Indeed, there is scarcely a human gesture in the poem which is accepted, or delighted in, or permitted any mysteries.

We are often told that the key moment occurs with the hyacinth girl episode in 'The Burial of the Dead'; and in a way it does, though the significance of this fragment has little to do with tracking down references to the Grail legend. What matters in these lines is that here is one human contact which *is* fertile of beauty and excitement. In human terms, however, it is clearly an expression of emotional failure; or, more precisely, of a failure to limit feeling to the human object that inspires it. It is not the girl's humanity that matters, so much as her power, being human, to release the speaker from his own humanity:

> *I could not*
> *Speak, and my eyes failed, I was neither*
> *Living nor dead, and I knew nothing,*
> *Looking into the heart of light, the silence.*

These are very beautiful lines, and they are central for what they tell us of Eliot's distaste not just for casual sex but, in *The Waste Land*, for all behaviour that is inescapably human. (It is significant that in 'The Game of Chess' the hyacinth garden experience is recalled in order to measure the widening distance between the speaker and his ageing Cleopatra; there is no way in which *she* can share in the fruits of the experience.) It is not so much that sex ought to be taken

more seriously, nor that—if taken seriously—it can offer a route to
certain worthy spiritual objectives. The poem's energy is not
directed, as it might have been, towards a deepening exploration of
the intuitions experienced with the hyacinth girl but concentrates
rather on the less arduous business of symptomatizing the condition
of those whose lives are undisturbed, or unenriched, by such intuitions. Commentators on *The Waste Land* have talked approvingly of
its telling condemnation of 'sex for the sake of sex'. But there is
surely as much lacking in Eliot's view of sex as there is in the relationships he presents for our pitying scrutiny. If any one of these
were less than extraordinarily dehumanized, we might have a more
worrying antithesis to ponder. What really troubles, though, is that
the poem aspires to some kind of final, representative wisdom on
these matters while at the same time excluding whole areas of experience which are vital to such wisdom. The offered choice is of
either a mystical 'transcending' of the body or what amounts to a
pornographic debasing of it. This is surely not the choice we are
faced with in reality.

No one in *The Waste Land*—though the poem is obsessed with
sexual behaviour ('A Game of Chess' and 'The Fire Sermon' are
concerned with little else)—actually enjoys sex. It is seen throughout
as a kind of enervated reflex, a set of tired, distracting compulsions
whose servants would as soon be free. The typist home at tea-time,
even though her sole function in the poem is as an erotic object, is
scrupulously not permitted even the dimmest erotic appeal. Quite
the opposite, in fact; her underwear repellently comprises 'combina-
tions', 'camisoles' and 'stays'. Her capitulation to the 'young man
carbuncular' is 'bored', 'tired', 'indifferent'—this is no passionate
folly, no excess of carnal zeal, no fun. The room is in tawdry dis-
order, the meal is eaten out of tins (why should *that* be so awful? and
do we really have to think of it as 'a kind of Grail Repast which the
Loathly Damsel has prepared'? [Grover Smith, p. 88]), the boy
friend has a bad complexion. The simple, nose-crinkling snobbish-
ness that underlies 'One of the low on whom assurance sits/As a silk
hat on a Bradford millionaire' cannot envisage a typist and a clerk

having any other kind of relationship. But then the most heroic seduction would stand little chance against the arms-length vocabulary which Eliot employs here: 'endeavours', 'encounters', 'requires', 'assaults' and so on; this is refrigerating language, prissily dignified, fastidiously embarrassed. In a similar way, 'By Richmond I raised my knees/Supine on the floor of a narrow canoe' seems to take more than legitimate satisfaction in its isolation of crude practicalities; one feels that in whatever spirit those knees were raised it would have made little difference to the way Eliot looked at them. As we have seen, though, no one in *The Waste Land* raises her knees in any other spirit than that of glum complaisance.

The typist episode, of course, is viewed through the blind eyes of Tiresias, 'old man with wrinkled dugs'. Indeed, this is the only point in the poem where the protagonist is explicitly identified. And Eliot's own note, that Tiresias is 'the most important personage in the poem, uniting all the rest' obliges us to regard him with a special interest—though not with quite the interest that Grover Smith takes in him. It has often been assumed that the usefulness of Tiresias is that he can stand for a universal, omniscient view of things—and this is no doubt the way Eliot wanted him to be regarded. In allowing that, of course, we are granting Eliot the same omniscience. But Tiresias is, after all, a freak. Old, blind, bisexual. Why should we take these characteristics to denote unusual wisdom (especially about sex) when they can more justifiably be taken to confess unusual ignorance. Mainly because the whole impersonal posture of the poem painstakingly discourages us from viewing any of it as vulnerably self-expressive, from attempting to detect any subjective centres. By adopting Tiresias as a key *persona*, Eliot implicitly invites us to modify the poem's judgements, to see them in perspective of Tiresias's disabilities—add to blindness and bisexuality an excessive literary sophistication and a vaguely transcendental horror of the flesh and we are hardly faced with the ideal equipment for impersonal jurisdiction. But Eliot's procedure in *The Waste Land* is, precisely, to proffer personal disabilities as impersonal talents, to allow emotional weaknesses to masquerade as moral strengths. With the

character of Tiresias, as with the hyacinth girl, the poem moves just
so far towards touching on what looks like a very deep and personal alienation, a simple, experienced inability to settle for the kind
of lives that other people settle for, but it quickly stiffens into anonymity and diagnosis. We are shown enough, however, of the poet's
personality for us to view with some distrust the sophistry he masks
it with.

Most studies of *The Waste Land* have taken it for granted that it is
written to a marvellously intricate plan, that Eliot is godlike in his
remote, clandestine machinations. Typical of much academic criticism is the assumption that whatever *is* in a poem belongs in it, as by
divine law. Eliot's notes, the information that Pound sub-edited the
poem, the opinion of Eliot's close friend, Conrad Aiken, that the
whole was made up fairly arbitrarily of bits and pieces which had
been around for years, the tediously demonstrated fact that none of
the interpretations is finally more convincing than the others and
that all have been obliged to embrace suspect ingenuities; none of
this has deterred the true disciple from his conviction that the work
is some kind of dense, elaborate miracle of form which it is the
poetry lover's humble, lengthy duty to attempt to document. But
the mysteries remain: just what is Phlebas the Phoenician doing in
the poem; had he not been there, would he have been missed? Are
Madame Sosostris's predictions really necessary, except to provide
the *appearance* of a general scheme? Just what does go on in Magnus
Martyr?

The clue that the Grail Legend is at the back of *The Waste Land*
has been a gift, of course, and its reverential treatment by the critics
has been sadly typical of their elementary reluctance to place any
faith in their own puzzlement. The Legend itself has a simple resonance—it treats of sickness and health, aridity and fertility, life and
death; it is rich with punishments and rewards, with crucial talis-
mans and cruel tests. It also has the advantage for scholars of existing
in many different versions, and its symbolism is complicatedly
diffused and multi-significant. None the less, Eliot could hardly be
said to have made its dramas clearer or more lively to a modern

reader. He does not select any single version and he is even ready to express his ignorance of, say, 'the exact constitution of the Tarot pack' (though finding that the Hanged Man 'fits his purpose' because it ties up in his mind with Frazer's Hanged God and also with the hooded figure on the road to Emmaus—the poem is altogether too fond of this kind of tenuous, loosely evocative kind of coincidence). He makes no effort to redramatize the legend in terms of its supposed modern significances, but rather treats it as a repository of primitive lore from which he can arbitrarily select some useful tokens. The legend itself, as a believed drama, remains colourfully dead. Eliot takes a kind of antiquarian interest in its symbolic paraphernalia, but its real attraction for him is less imaginative than theoretical; it represents a particular kind of spiritual enterprise, one which could assimilate sexuality to sacred ends. The chief failure is that Eliot employs the legend merely to signal the idea; by using fragments of its symbolism he is able to hold in the reader's mind a notion of some ideal type of religio-sexual feeling. The legend thus supplies a bogus specificity to the criteria by which modern humans have been found guilty and disgusting.

And this is typical of the poem's overall strategy. To put it crudely, we are given too much judgement and too little evidence. And what evidence we do get seems rigged. But why? Answering that question—or even allowing it to impinge—would surely have produced a richer and more humane text for the Grover Smiths to ponder.

1970

Louis MacNeice

It is not surprising that Louis MacNeice's reputation has survived the 'thirties' rather more comfortably than those of his colleagues in the famous quartet; his guilt-ridden perplexity in the face of those fiercely clear-cut obligations has easily attracted a generation of post-war poets for whom such bafflement represents the proper limits of political involvement and whose intermittent nostalgia for more vigorous public contexts can be quenched by his sharply documented local colour. The prestige of the Inner Debate can rarely have been higher than it is today, when to recognize that 'the contradictions cover such a range' is about as deep in practical wisdom as most of our poets care to wade. A poetry like MacNeice's which is so persistently dogged by honest doubt, which wavers at such intimate lengths between such dismal opposites, can be expected to have a ready appeal. But to accept this as a full characterization of MacNeice's achievement is to under-emphasize the very gifts which he himself spent so much time suppressing and apologizing for; it is to be too solemn about a poet who could never finally accept that he 'loved the surface but lacked the core'.

'He cannot be a politician and he will not be a reactionary' lamented Geoffrey Grigson in *New Verse*, sentencing MacNeice for being less assertive and more sorry for himself than Auden, and this problem of personal integrity—how to maintain it, how to distinguish it from self-indulgence, lassitude and flippancy—is a central, debilitating one in his immediately pre-war verse. It is as if MacNeice's development in the direction of profuse, superficial abandonment and whimsicality (which is discernible in *Blind Fireworks* and is condemned by Grigson as Sitwellian but for its neatness) got suddenly arrested by the public calamities of his time and forced into new, hardly congenial, directions—into abstract discourse, rhetorical self-examination.

It is interesting that in this first volume MacNeice constantly treats of visual experience which is unintelligibly (if engrossingly) fluid and confused; he confronts a glittering, opalescent universe in a wholly submissive and amiable manner. Poem after poem opens on a note of tranquil decline; 'the quietude of the soft wind', 'Trains came threading quietly through my dozing childhood', 'In this evening room there is no stir, no fuss', 'The room is all a stupid quietness', 'In a between world . . . the old cat . . . sleeps on the verge of nullity' and so on. It is from a similarly drowsy 'between world' that MacNeice watches his random experience fragment and dissolve. Time passes, the view changes, these poems seem to say. The poet's intrusion on the cycle is marginal, almost photographic, rarely rhetorical or analytic, never profoundly disturbed.

What is charming in these early poems is a fractional immediacy of perception, a developed gift for projecting a momentary visual complex (a gift that made MacNeice wary of grand systems; see the post-war 'Plurality' for an interesting, if leadenly expressed, background to all this) and a passive liveliness to the sheer plenitude and variety of human experience.

It is easy to see how gifts of this kind could be made to seem irresponsible and trivial, but it is in them that one can discover the source of MacNeice's most brilliant passages of social reportage and also of the self-consciousness that enervates such large stretches of his subsequent work. There are a number of poems in his 1931–5 collection ('Morning Sun', for instance, and 'Snow') which are quite confidently in his first manner, and there is a welcome extension of interest to urban industrial situations; the note of doom which in *Blind Fireworks* is fairly mechanically borne in by the ticking clock is here more firmly localized and insisted on. But there is a new note of guilt that

> *We jump from picture to picture and cannot follow*
> *The living curve that is breathlessly the same.*

He answers such qualms by asserting that he could not naturally write in any other way; the point is, though, that he is already writing differently—a new manner, prosy and argumentative, has been adopted; in this case to rebut prosy argument:

> *The tide comes in and goes out again, I do not want*
> *To be always stressing either its flux or its permanence.*
> *I do not want to be a tragic or philosophic chorus*
> *But to keep my eye only on the nearer future*
> *And after that let the sea flow over us.*

From this point two distinct, almost antithetical styles are allowed to co-exist in his work. The love of bright particulars persists and is given important body by the socio-political materials which it begins to assimilate. Throughout the 'Eclogues', the 1936–8 volume, and the best passages (Parts 5 to 8, particularly) of *Autumn Journal* there is a range and accuracy of observation, a lively grasp of the frenetic bored excess of a threatened social order, which are really admirable. Predictably, it is the scope and variety of social experience, the detail of its surface, that delights him; he alternates between moods of jaunty 'bravado in the face of time', of ironic sumptuousness, and of flat, menacing reportage:

> *Nelson is stone and Johnny Walker moves his*
> *Legs like a cretin over Trafalgar Square.*
> *And in the Corner House the carpet-sweepers*
> *Advance between the tables after crumbs*
> *Inexorably, like a tank battalion*
> *In answer to the drums.*

> *In Tottenham Court Road the tarts and negroes*
> *Loiter beneath the lights*
> *And the breeze gets colder as on so many other*
> *September nights.*
> *A smell of French bread in Charlotte Street, a rustle*
> *Of leaves in Regent's Park*

> *And suddenly from the Zoo I hear a sea-lion*
> *Confidently bark.*

But if the thirties climate matured MacNeice's bright, documentary style it also encouraged the development of his prosy analysis. The problem of his own personal involvement in what he saw could not be evaded and MacNeice became obliged to stand at the centre of his work in a confessional stance that did not suit him but which he never completely abandoned. His doctrine of the poet as extension of the ordinary man was not vanity but a way of burying his personality in the kind of plural activity he could handle. He believed that the poet should remain elastic in his sympathies whatever the pressures on him to propagandize; his reaction against the 'esoteric' poetry of Eliot did not mean that he chose instead a legislating or civilizing role for the poet but simply that he must write out of experience which was generally available and interesting. For this purpose his poetry of appearances could work very well. But the detachment, the range of acceptance which it presupposed was difficult to preserve. Credentials had to be shown, the surfaces had to be probed.

It is in attempting this that MacNeice is at his weakest. The devitalized ambivalence of, say, Parts 2 and 3 of *Autumn Journal* is typical; the conflicts he writes about are real and important ones and his motives are worthy, but the structure of his argument is limp and half-heartedly protracted. One is conscious primarily of an enormous failure of energy. Part 2 opens with the poet suicidally inert. The desire for 'oblivion' and 'Pure Not-being' seems to underlie much of what happens in the journal; it is never clear if this malaise results from the insoluble issues of commitment that face him, if it is a personal failure in love that causes it, or if it is to be seen as symptomatic of the total uneasiness of the time. One wonders about this because the public and personal strands of the poem never work out into complementary levels of concern but are often entangled and dramatically harmful to each other:

> *I wonder whether anything is worth*

C

> *The eyelid opening and the mind recalling.*

He attempts to shake off this mood by what is a somewhat frigid affirmation of social responsibility:

> *I must go out tomorrow as the others do*
> *And build the falling castle.*

It is between these two attitudes that the argument in *Autumn Journal* moves, and at much this level of intellectual and verbal distinction. MacNeice seems trapped by his own candour and one can sense the relief with which he emerges from these troughs into the company of places and people in Part 5.

In his war-time poems, MacNeice attempts to synthesize the rhetorical and documentary aspects of his work in a series of anec-dotal character-poems ('The Conscript', 'The Mixer', 'The Satirist') but these are too complacently punch-lined, their solutions intrude too glaringly and, worst, they are pale imitations of Auden. The tight, witty accent is largely abandoned and where it is attempted— as in 'Brother Fire', 'Bar-Room Matins' etc.—it seems tricksy and hollow. A poem like 'Trolls' (written after an air-raid in April 1941) suggests that at this stage MacNeice has reached something of an impasse. On the one hand there is imitation of early gusto:

> *Skittle-alley horse-play, congurgitation . . . they don't*
> *know what they are doing*
> *All they can do is stutter and lurch, riding their hobby, grinding*
> *Their hob-nails into our brains, into the domed*
> *Head where the organ-music lingers:*

Pretty Polly won't die yet and on the other, there is this kind of enfeebled speculation:

> *Death has a look of finality;*
> *We think we lose something but if it were not for*
> *Death we should have nothing to lose, existence*
> *Because unlimited would merely be existence*
> *Without incarnate value. The trolls can occasion*

> *Our death but they are not able*
> *To use it as we can use it.*

Regrettably it is this second manner which he chooses to develop in the long poems, 'The Stygian Banks', 'The Kingdom' and 'The Window' which close his *Collected Poems 1925–48*; the paradoxes here seem even less urgent than they did in *Autumn Journal* and his counter-blows on behalf of the fluid instant are wearily automatic:

> *Far from perfect*
> *Presumes perfection* where? *A catechism in drums*
> *Asseverate day-long, night-long; Glory is what?*
> *A question! . . . Now it is Spring.*

If this seems to be the most depressing period of MacNeice's career it is because one senses that he has finally sacrificed his real gifts; the Wurlitzer rhythms of 'Bagpipe Music' could not seem more remote, the lyrical surrenders of *Blind Fireworks* are remembered as the irresponsibilities of youth. All that remains is a defeated plotting of absurdity.

Something of this persists to *Autumn Sequel* (1954), a long poem in *terza rima*, although here there is more concern for particulars. The work has its lively moments, but MacNeice still seems unhappy in the responsible first person and much of his material seems random, private or dull; a film-script is worked on, the office is loathed, bargains are made, museums are visited, friends die, and so little seems to matter. But one can see that it could all have been more interesting had MacNeice not felt bound to penetrate his incident in the way he does; the weighty, prolix pondering of rather slight events cannot compensate for their triviality and often exposes and exaggerates it. There can be little doubt that the B.B.C. encouraged MacNeice even further towards speculation and discourse and away from his lyric past. The work is admittedly rhetorical in conception but this doesn't help; it remains dead on the page, and the gossip and the puns do little to enliven it:

> *Leaving the colleges then and their half-remembered*

> *Hobsnobberies, which echoed my own voice,*
> *I make my way through warmly umbered embered*
>
> *Foliage to catch a bus in search of Boyce*
> *Who lives in a village in a seasoned home,*
> *Keeping his head and exercising choice*
>
> *And titivating his garden.*

It is noticeable that in *Visitations* (1957) and *Solstices* (1961) MacNeice was able to rediscover much of his old concentration and vitality, and to withdraw into the background of his work. In these he is no longer so prone to 'mark the spot/Meticulously in black and white' but is more directly susceptible once more to 'whatever glints'. There are still poems in which he seems to lose his nerve after a riotous first stanza and relapses into frozen paradox but on the whole one senses a welcome access of vigour and invention. This is true also of the volume that was published a fortnight after his death, *The Burning Perch*. His *Budgie* once more attitudinizes entertainingly; that it does so on a burning perch is not ignored but nor is it laboriously over-emphasized. Throughout the book the old paradoxes are seen to be inexorable, and thus nonsensical or terrifying, or both; undebatable finally, but still to be spoken of:

> *So bandage his eyes since he paid to come in but somehow forgot*
> *To follow the others out—and now there is no way out*
> *Except that his inturned eyes before he falls may show him*
> *Some nettled orchard, tousled hedge, some garden even*
> *Where flowers, whether they boast or insinuate, whisper*
>   *or shout,*
> *Still speak a living language.*

1963

William Empson

The tendency for critics to be patronizing about Empson's later poetry while extravagantly praising his early work can probably be traced back to F. R. Leavis's complaint in his 1950 Retrospect in *New Bearings* that the young poet whom he had so enthusiastically launched in 1932 had (with, one assumes, his second volume and the poems since) failed to develop satisfactorily. Leavis is very oblique about this failure: in very general terms he attributes it to 'sophistication', or 'that air of knowing one's way about: in short, that preoccupation with intellectuality and the externals of profundity and subtlety'. This sophistication Leavis sees as a property of the thirties climate in which 'the natural appetite for kudos is not chastened by contact with mature standards, and in which fixed immaturity can take itself for granted'.

It is difficult to be more vague than this but what sense can be got out of it seems fairly inaccurate as a characterization of Empson's development. Empson starts out as a highly sophisticated maker of puzzles, preoccupied with intellectual jesting and the kudos that pointless dexterity so often invites in academic circles and it is as a consequence of finding this flashy style so early that he responds so grudgingly to the political situations of the thirties. In a sense, it is the thirties and their terrible public events that expose the narrowness of Empson's early manner and demand from him the handful of poems, stanzas and single lines that argue his considerable potential.

No amount of misleading talk about Donne can escape the fact that the bulk of Empson's early verse is unattractively obscure; his wildly ingenious parallels and contrasts rarely seem obligatory; they are relished for their outrageousness, their anti-inevitability. He will often lead off from some bizarre or pedantic situation he has come upon in his reading or his crossword puzzles—art-galleries, jugglers

whose apples are rotten, scorpions that are suicidal under glass etc.—
and on a principle of high-class free-association he will improvise.
This means often a crabwise extension through its parallels of his
original situation (the parallels being equally odd) and a final, absor-
bent image of the absolute. A number of poems begin and end in
this way. They open charmingly—an eccentric perception is placed
before us, or exposed to Empson's virtuosity. Rarely is this perception dramatized or given vitality in its own terms, nor is it often
made seriously into an agent of abstract worries. It rarely seems to
have been *chosen* because of some precise function that it can pecu-
liarly perform, or because it can discover something of an important
experience that the poet has already had. What one is called upon to
admire is the skill that can so fetchingly graft the quaintly esoteric
on to the traditionally portentous experience.

The more arbitrary the initial situation the better, almost, because
then Empson's teasing out of its relations, his bland extension of it
into the cosmic terms we have stock respect for, will seem cleverer.
But in the end it is this arbitrary aspect (this feeling that the poem
might as well have opened differently since it was destined to end
this way) that infects so many of these early poems with a lethal
germ of silliness. One often feels that the improvisation could go on
indefinitely, that it is only by dexterously imposing on his promis-
cuous Fancy these absolute limits that Empson can get the process to
stop.

Plenum and Vacuum opens with the scorpions who 'kill themselves
when put under glass and frightened with fire':

> *Delicate goose-step of penned scorpions*
> *Patrols its weal under glass-cautered bubble;*
> *Postpones, fire-cinct, their suicide defiance,*
> *Pierced carapace stung in mid vault of bell.*

'Delicate goose-step' is a neat perception; its resonance is limited by
observation, by respect for the physical particular that it primarily
refers to. But 'weal' seems clumsily wrong, partly because it is
somewhat archaic and unnatural, but mostly because it seems to

have been pondered and placed without the same direct reference to concrete experience that 'delicate goose-step' has. The notes confirm this impression; they direct one to consider 'weal' as 'the scar of a burn, made as a glass was, the ground still under the control of their commonwealth, the circle of the glass rim, and the gain of death'. What disturbs here is not that it does not mean all these things—it surely can be made to—but that we can only give it any kind of assent on these narrow terms. (Also, of course, it could mean other things; it could be read, for instance, as a pun on 'wheel' and thus be seen to introduce notions of fate, to describe the circular motion of the scorpions—with parade-ground overtones that would fit in with 'patrols' and so on.) No single, or primary recognition of the word is forceful enough; it needs this apologizing apparatus of ambiguity. The discovery of these other meanings is not, however, a revelation of a genuine resonance that toughens a surface activity we have already grasped and enjoyed by giving it a precisely worked out depth. In a sense, all four of Empson's meanings must be held at surface level, and this merely intensifies one's discomfort and distracts one from the poem's action. The notes often work in this way, exacerbating rather than soothing one's first qualms, and even after long acquaintance they do not work themselves into the poems and become dispensable. Indeed, their whole manner suggests they have been built to last.

The scorpions remain imprisoned in the first stanza; the new situation that is introduced by stanza two—the effect of screaming on the eyes and the mechanism our bodies have for mitigating this— is not so much a legitimate next step in the argument as a fresh start, a parallel example. The scorpions are registered as example one and discarded (this can easily be done because they were never really meant to be *real* scorpions; they are like most of concrete life in these poems, 'for the sake of argument') and an infinite number of new examples can—presumably—now be introduced. The intellectual content is not developed by the examples, it is merely common to them. Therefore, in order to truncate a potentially limitless activity, there is in stanza three a mechanical shift to the abstract, the limits of intellectual experience. The poem ends when, literally, it cannot go any further. That is to say, the laws by which it ends are not built into it, but are the laws by which anything ends. Thus, in stanza three one has: Matter, space, firmament, Heaven, rainbows, Styx, Hell. This grand finale does not seem a compulsory fruition of the drama which stanza one seemed to promise; as much as anything it is a way of making that drama more eccentric than it really needs to be, just as the drama itself makes the conclusion seem less solemnly conceptual.

This kind of strategy is evident even in the poems where the cosmic machinery is more generously diffused. There is always this desire, it seems, to employ a grandly abstract vocabulary (a compound of traditional—pagan and Christian—world-concepts and modern cosmology) without being caught looking too solemn with it. The congested syntax is useful here and so is the odd note of whimsy. Empson's zestful pedantry, his involved argumentative structures, his abstruse situations out of science and literature—these behave as a kind of quasi-particularization.

The many instances of cumbersome flippancy in early Empson (though he never gets rid of the habit altogether) do little to encourage one to the labour of exegesis in less obviously vulnerable areas:

> *That over-all that Solomon should wear*
> *Gives these no cope who cannot know of care.*
> *They have no gap to spare that they should share*
> *The rare calyx we stare at in despair.*
>
> *They have no other that they should compare.*
> *Their arch of promise the wide Heaviside layer*
> *They rise above a vault into the air.*

This manner is carried to absurdly boring lengths in 'Poem about a Ball in the Nineteenth Century' and it offers a striking instance of that sterile naughtiness which helps to disable more ambitious poems. There are jarring hints of it in 'To an Old Lady' (where, interestingly, the effect of his excellent last stanza is disturbed by one's feeling that the 'stars' and the 'darkness' are primarily to be grasped as the final flourish of a cosmological conceit): 'Project her no projectile, plan nor man it', 'Confident, finds no confine on her sphere'. The rhythm is gruellingly ugly. There is a leisured vanity at the back of such awkwardnesses and it seriously qualifies the whole tone of the piece.

Much has been made of Empson's interest in science and it is often suggested that his is an important modern achievement because he has managed to appropriate a scientific vocabulary for poetry. But has he, in fact, made this vocabulary more available? Hart Crane's comment is worth noting: 'Unless poetry can absorb the machine, i.e. acclimatize it as naturally and casually as trees, cattle, galleons, castles and all other human associations of the past, then poetry has failed of its full contemporary function.' Empson's verse does not assimilate scientific experience in this way; it employs a frame of scientific reference, certainly, but it does not attempt to familiarize the language by making it directly confront experience of a non-scientific kind. The unfamiliarity is in fact recognized and exploited by the poet; it is precisely the remoteness of the idiom that commends it to him. One cannot go on pretending, as many puzzled, friendly critics do, that 'Bacchus' never happened; clearly Empson was heavily committed to it over a considerable period of time. It is the predictable outcome of his early sophistication, 'his air of knowing his way around', and he continues to reprint it. Empson's early manner finally seems arid because it operates without much reference to concrete human experience; there is a sharp limit to the situations, relationships and cadences that can vitalize it. The contemporary situations that Eliot makes poetry out of are trivialized in Empson to jests about Douglas Fairbanks. For this feat he has been variously applauded. As Charles Madge puts it: 'Thirdly, references from the contemporary scene—underground trains, tooth-paste, Douglas Fairbanks; it was this capacity to assimilate the non-traditional which F. R. Leavis applauded more than twenty years ago.'

The Gathering Storm, as its title implies, is specifically about the contemporary scene and the political forces that were a threatening feature of it. Some of the poems in it appeared in the anthology *New Signatures* which was committed to a 'symbolism which happens to be of an exceptionally wide validity' and whose editor announced that 'the poems in this book represent a clear reaction against esoteric poetry in which it is necessary for the reader to catch each recondite allusion'. It would be inaccurate to suggest that Empson shared these sentiments, or that he had much real interest in the 'popular poetry' which Michael Roberts thought possible. He had no intention of being solemn, even about China, and in poems like 'Your Teeth' ('Critics often say that modern poetry retires into an ivory tower, doesn't try to make contact with a reader, or escapes facing the problems of the time. I try to defend it by saying that there is a good deal of defence in ordinary life'), 'Aubade' ('Tell me again about Europe and her pains/Who's tortured by the drought, who by the rains?'), 'Autumn on Nan-Yueh' ('Besides, I do not really like/The Verses about/Up the Boys/The revolutionary romp'), and 'Just a Smack at Auden', he is clearly out to dissociate himself from the movement which had said of him (in *New Verse*) 'The clever fellows must wait to show off some other day.' The weakness of his overtly 'political' poems ('Reflection from Rochester', 'Courage Means Running') is that in them he seems too aware of the conventions of their literary environment; he is somewhat too anxious to take an original stand, and this anxiety gets seriously between the poem and its subject and confuses its tone. His approach is non-patriotic, anti-alarmist, but coldly respectful of the threatened enormities, and his manner of presenting this displays an uneasy wavering between the didactic and the whimsical; in trying too hard to be moderate where others are intemperate, to be universal where others are cheaply contemporary, and so on, Empson too often appears merely unconcerned. Partly, this impression arises out of the abstraction of his language (in 'Courage Means Running', for example, one has 'fear', 'courage', 'knowledge', 'purpose', 'emotion', 'hope', 'truth', 'pleasure', 'pain', 'self-respect', 'patience' etc.)

and his difficult syntax (it is difficult in a brusque rather than pedantic way, as if he grudges the topics his attention), but most often it is the uncertainty of his tone. There is a High Table smirk behind such lines as

> To take fear as the measure
> May be the measure of self-respect. Indeed
> As the operative clue in seeking treasure
> Is normally trivial. . . .

which insures against what follows being taken as too committedly straightfaced.

> As to be hurt is petty, and to be hard
> Stupidity: as the economists raise
> Bafflement to a boast we all take as guard.

There are uncertainties of this kind in a number of poems ('Aubade', for instance, which has all the makings of a good and inclusive political poem done in terms of a personal situation, is constantly worried by hints that it is not to be taken to heart) and the strands can be developed in the direction of—on the one hand—the polished ironies of 'Ignorance of Death' (which is successful because it is thoroughly sure of what it is supposed to be doing—there are no artfully dropped pronouns, no word-plays disguising its motives) or—on the other—'Autumn on Nan-Yueh', a literary polemic that seems to have been thrown together in a fit of irritated self-defence. Astringent aloofness from the whole thing or messy engagement in the literary squabbles about how to treat it; neither alternative generates powerful or convincing poetry—often because they are getting in each other's way, but also because they are too deliberately attitudes for an occasion. On the whole one prefers the relaxed sardonics to the chatter, and 'Ignorance of Death' is more convincing than the obviously 'political' poems because its control is given a tragic edge: there is a pressure of personal feeling behind it and one is conscious that its ironic poise is achieved at some considerable expense and is precarious:

> *Otherwise I feel very blank upon this topic,*
> *And think that though important, and proper for*
> > *anyone to bring up,*
> *It is one that most people should be prepared*
> > *to be blank upon.*

This is a note that Empson often strikes—but too rarely sustains—and it is his most powerful one. It creates, broadly, a conflict between the habits of the sophisticated intelligence and the fears that it cannot dispel; the more confidence placed in the intellect, the more tragically moving is the discovery of its limitations felt to be, and yet, paradoxically, it is precisely these habits that can promise endurance of the discovery. The ending of 'Missing Dates' has just this threatened control:

> *It is the poems you have lost, the ills*
> *From missing dates, at which the heart expires.*
> *Slowly the poison the whole blood stream fills.*
> *The waste remains, the waste remains and kills.*

This is superb; the distress finely modulated, the voice wholly original and the reference to experience powerfully frontal. It is in lines like these and in poems like 'Manchouli', 'Let it Go', 'The Beautiful Train', and the translations from Miss Hatakeyama (in particular, 'The Small Bird to the Big'—a poem it is sadly difficult to imagine Empson admitting to having written; the self-exposure can always be blamed on the original) that Empson is memorably at his best, not at all sophisticated.

1963

All American

A few weeks before William Carlos Williams' *Pictures from Breughel* was published here in 1964, the *New Statesman* warned its readers that American was really a foreign language. Williams would have been delighted. It has been his insistence on the special burdens and excitements of the truly American poet that has been responsible for his notorious neglect in this country—a neglect that is now being over-hastily repaired. Aside from anthologies, magazines and the efforts of enterprising American distributors, *Pictures from Breughel* represented his first English appearance since Elkin Matthews brought out *The Tempers* in 1913.

Williams's reputation in the United States is currently at its height and in reverence to his memory all really ambitious young American experimenters are breaking their lines according to strange, secret dictates from the breath and pulse-rate. At the back of this 'Williams revival', though, there is too a resurgence of Williams's ambition for a thoroughly emancipated American verse—boring the English may well become one of its more positive strategies. Although Williams has been published here by courtesy of his imitators and vulgarizers, it would be a mistake to entangle his work too closely with what they have made of it.

At the same time, one has to acknowledge that it is difficult to be an American poet without at some level getting on to terms with Williams's irritable prescriptions. Donald Hall's recent Penguin *Contemporary American Poetry* defined the dilemma neatly, locating two clear lines of development—the first, and most firmly en-trenched during the last thirty years, an American verse that func-tions as an aspect of the English tradition, and is subservient to it; the second, Williams's 'colloquial line', a deliberate rejection of European assumptions, a self-conscious effort towards the distinguishably American.

It was just this sort of dilemma that Williams himself faced nearly fifty years ago. Whether or not the choice was, or is, really necessary is surely questionable but Williams felt it could not be avoided and strenuously chose America; apart from anything else it is in these terms that his career is instructive. 'Before meeting Ezra Pound is like B.C. and A.D.,' Williams has written, and it was out of his encounters with the modernist enterprise as interpreted and developed by Eliot and Pound that his notion of 'the American grain' developed. Before Pound, he was writing 'Keatsian sonnets', an imitation of *Endymion*, and dabbling in Whitmanesque; what Pound gave him was the elementary principle which he was to maintain throughout his life—the direct particularity sloganized in his celebrated, 'Say it! No ideas but in things.' Williams appeared in Pound's 1914 *Des Imagistes* anthology and one imagines that up to the appearance of *Kora in Hell* (1920) Pound was able to think of him as 'Little Bill (i.e. W.C.W., as distinct from Big Bill, W.B.Y.)'. After *Kora in Hell*, though—its Prologue mounts a vigorous attack on the international school of modernism as led by Pound and Eliot (on the offering of 'parodies of the middle ages, Dante and Langue D'oc . . . as the best in U.S. poetry')—Pound began to write of Williams as an 'old village cut-up', a 'dago immigrant' whose Americanism was not a little posed and juvenile. To Pound, absorbed in his recreations of the proper tradition, it was 'doubly lamentable that the two halves of what might have been a fairly decent poet shd. be sequestered and divided by the buttocks of the arse-wide Atlantic ocean'. As for Williams, he had come to regard the modern movement as enslaved by the foreign influences which he felt had disfigured America from the start. *The Waste Land* was the final betrayal; Eliot, he wrote, had given the poem back to the academics . . . 'I had to watch him carry my world with him, the fool, to the enemy.'

In his *In the American Grain* (1925) Williams attempted to define the American task in more detail and to direct the objective manner to its peculiar, national purposes. The value of the concrete, unprejudiced image, he maintained, was that it offered a means of discovering a 'primary impetus in the local conditions' of America, of getting on to direct, and at least visual, terms with the 'hard, sardonic, truculent mass of the New World'. American history had begun with 'murder and enslavement, not with discovery'; as a nation it had been born of a desire to 'huddle, to protect' transplanted prejudices and ambitions. The Puritans had fashioned it to their narrow, theological pattern—'instead of growing, they looked black at the world'—and its artists had let it be 'painted over, smeared', had sought to accommodate its experience to the assumptions of their imported cultures. What 'wellnigh no man of distinction' saw was 'a world of great beauty and ripest blossom' which had yet to be experienced in its own terms. Only by eliminating the sophistications that might interfere between the alert eye and its newly discovered object could the poet approach America for what she was, a local mystery.

There is a considerable body of Williams's work which is as thinly documentary as this theory seems to promise; the surface of some local experience is neatly denoted and then left, merely available, a confirmation rather than an insight. The endeavour is quasi-scientific and seeks no surprises. The attitude to nature is one of fussy homage, a cold gratitude for its varied attributes. As R. P. Blackmur has said, Williams 'isolates and calls attention to what we are already in possession of'; much of the time he demonstrates those gifts of observation which one placidly expects from a rather average novelist. It is in these, the most cryptic, deadly factual of his poems—and he never stopped accumulating them—that the incongruity between the grandiose aspirations of his theory and the trivial effects of its literal practice is most sharply felt; one longs for some of that despised 'lyrical interference' and to remind Williams that in order to really respect a tree the poet does not have to be wooden, and that in order to 'discover' America in the objective-visual sense these poems imply one really needs to have committees of cold-eyed observers deployed throughout the continent. Not that one would then have poetry; the point is that Williams's excuse for not writing the lyric poetry

which he was so well equipped for was that he was engaged on some
kind of functional research programme. As it is, of course, his catalogue of suburban views gives us the low-down on what he arbitrarily
had to hand but makes a fairly glancing dent in the 'hard, sardonic
truculent mass' he claimed it to be penetrating.

The most ambitious upshot of Williams's documentary zeal is the
long poem *Paterson*, which was first 'finished' in 1951 when Book 4
appeared. (In 1958, Book 5 was added, to encompass—in Williams's
words—'the many changes . . . in me and the world', and he was
planning a sixth book during the months before his death in 1963.)
It is not surprising that *Paterson* turned out to be interminable. Its
progress, since the appearance of Book 1 in 1946, was more and
more in the direction of what Randall Jarrell called 'the organization
of irrelevance', and it grew progressively more haphazard and self-
indulgent in its pursuit of 'a particular history'. The general effort of
Paterson is to unfold an individual sensibility in terms of its environment, local, historical and cultural. 'I searched for a city', Williams
wrote, 'one that I knew. It couldn't be New York, not anything as
big as a metropolis', and perhaps the first limitation of the poem is
that its locale is selected not because it offers an urban complex
which is representative of modern America but rather because
Williams felt it to have an 'important colonial history'; it invited
further excavations in the American grain.

In effect, this historicizing motive is what finally seems to enfeeble
the poem's structure, permitting a remorseless particularity whose
single cumulative meaning—that people have curious, entangled
pasts which they ought to know about and have a language for—
could have been more firmly demonstrated in a tenth of the space.
Even though some of the more charming passages in *Paterson* are the
prose accounts which Williams unearths from the local Historical
Society, it is never clear on what principle he is selecting and posi-
tioning them. The persistent question is, why this piece of engaging
trivia, and not another? In the same way, the personal letters that
appear from time to time usually have some interest in isolation but
most of the time it is difficult to see what they are doing in a poem.

It is even hard to determine whether or not they are real letters. One group in particular, those from 'C' that appear throughout Book 2, are desolate and embittered, and very moving, written to the poet by a woman who has overrated his regard for her and who is now ruthlessly examining her every wound; these letters dominate the book, and yet seem quite separate from it. If Williams wrote them, he has written a dramatic masterpiece; if not, and it seems fairly certain that he didn't, then who is 'C' and ought she to be flourished in this pointless way? Curiously enough, the depth and insight of her self-examination has the effect of making Williams's own confessions seem very thin and mannered.

But perhaps the basic point behind this endless accumulation, these fragments of utterly inconclusive evidence, is that an exploratory enterprise of this kind—if it is to be honest—has to be enthralled by whatever is factual, and that to select and manipulate is to disfigure; certainly the random piling up of detritus is almost bound to have some pathetic weight, and very often *Paterson* is moving for the simple reason that its materials *are* arbitrary. The history builds up and it is the fugitive detail that excites; by contrast Williams's own speculations about art and usury seem to have a good many more obvious ideas than curious, sad things.

Nevertheless, *Paterson* was intended to be read as a unified long poem and as such it must be judged a failure, probably an irresponsible one. The second reason Williams had for choosing the town of Paterson was, he said, that it has 'a river . . . the Passaic . . . and the Falls', which he could use as a spine for his epic. It is revealing to recall just how easy he thought it was going to be: 'This was my river and I was going to use it. I took the river as it followed its course down to the sea; all I had to do was to follow it and I had a poem.' Williams could hardly have voted for a more permissive regime, and it is only in Book 1 that the actual shape of Paterson, what it feels like to live there, exerts any central control; elsewhere, and with accelerating abandon, the river spills more or less where he pleases, sloppily emblematic—neither river nòr the agent of any special wisdom.

D

If Williams's American mission was mostly little more than a liability, there were ways in which it was of positive value to him. His best poems are those that neither document nor theorize (Williams is a far more abstract writer than he is usually given credit for, and on social and aesthetic issues he could be staggeringly muddled and boring) but derive directly from his experience as husband or father, and from his work as a small-town doctor. There is an obvious sense in which the scientific education which Pound deplored in Williams was an essential factor behind his trust in the pure, clinical act, and his work brought him into contact with a range of suffering which, he saw, the scalpel could not touch. In poems like 'The Widow's Lament in Springtime' say, or 'To Waken an Old Lady', his concrete materials are intensified to metaphor by a difficult, finely tentative, compassion; here it is the curiously bitten-off warmth of feeling that is recognizably American, and Williams's visual exactness is not experiment—it measures, rather, a superb, threatened restraint. All that Williams had so painstakingly learned of his environment comes into play, but is seen to operate dynamically from a centre of deep emotional involvement:

> *Old age is*
> *a flight of small*
> *cheeping birds*
> *skimming*
> *bare trees*
> *above a snow glaze.*
> *Gaining and failing*
> *they are buffeted*
> *by a dark wind.*
> *But what?*
> *On harsh weedstalks*
> *the flock has rested.*
> *The snow*
> *is covered with broken*
> *seedhusks*

> *and the wind tempered*
> *by a shrill piping of plenty.*

Even in this, one of Williams's least eccentrically shaped poems,
there is an obvious challenge to our formal assumptions; rather
more than his Americanist content it has been Williams's technical
individuality that has tended to alienate the English reader. Williams
formulated his position most fully during his association with the
Objectivists of the early thirties; together with Louis Zukofsky,
Charles Reznikoff and George Oppen, he organized and financed
the Objectivist Press which in 1935 brought out his *Collected Poems*.
Something of an Imagist revival was in progress; Glenn Hughes
brought out an Imagist anthology in 1930 and his book, *Imagism and
the Imagists*, in 1931. Williams and the Objectivists took the opportunity to dissociate their efforts from those of the Imagists which,
according to Williams, had been 'useful in ridding the field of verbiage' but had had 'no formal necessity'. 'There is no such thing as
free verse!' he declared, echoing Eliot, 'Verse is a measure of some
sort.' He went on to attempt a definition of this 'measure of some
sort' that would escape the dead metrical count and present itself as
an exclusive vehicle for the American idiom:

> the rule of counted syllables . . . has become tiresome to my ear
> . . . [they] have become entirely divorced from the beat, that is
> the measure. The musical pace proceeds without them. Therefore
> the measure, . . . having got rid of the words, which held it down,
> is returned to the *music*. The words, having been freed, have been
> allowed to run all over the map. . . . This has amounted to no
> more than no discipline at all. But if we keep in mind the *tune*
> which the lines (not necessarily the words) make in our ears, we
> are ready to proceed.

He goes on to give an instance of the kind of tune which his lines
make in his ears, and he relates his 'measure' to the action of his
breath while he is in the act of writing. The conclusion of his experiment is something of a give-away: 'You may not agree with my
ear, but that is the way I count the line.' It is this necessary qualifica-

tion that makes his systematizing seem rather pointless; in the end it
is the lucky ear that wins the prize. This, of course, must be partly
true of all poetry that does not limit its performance to the demands
of an agreed metrical vice. Where Williams goes wrong, though, is
not in systematizing the subjective, but in asserting so finally that
there can be *no* agreement in such matters. To astound our hoary
metrical preconceptions is one thing; to disturb the way in which
we've agreed to shape our syntax is a rather more difficult enterprise
and one that needs to be handled with tremendous integrity. Now
and then, Williams's 'open syntax' can present a pleasing range of
ambiguity; by omitting punctuation and carving up anticipated
sentence structures, he can allow his parts of speech to enjoy three or
four relations at once (an excellently academic aim). At worst the
method permits a puzzling kind of fun, and it is in this spirit that
Williams too often seems to handle it:

> *whom I myself*
> *ignorant*
> *as I was taught*
>
> *to read the poems*

By releasing 'ignorant as I was' from its parenthetic station, he un-
folds more possibilities than we are likely to feel disposed to juggle
with, and he effects not a specific criticism or expansion of his surface meaning, but a grinning diminution of its force. A gift for
campus teasers, possibly, but nothing much to do with poetry. And
not, in the end, anything like as clever as it looks.

One often feels this, that Williams's private measure not only
assaults the traditional metric but also the basic, involuntary habits
of ordinary speech; poetry should always be questioning these
habits, but it ought also to be rooted in them, respectfully. One
would need statistics, I suppose, but to take an obvious instance: it is
not ordinary practice to introduce a pause between a noun and its
definite article, not unless one wishes to suggest, say, hesitation, and
then—the noun having finally been pounced on—resolution.

Williams certainly seems to recognize this and often exploits his
line-breaks for this purpose, to imply a kind of total tentativeness, or
bewilderment in his approach to experience (his 'Asphodel, that
Greeny Flower', with its long, halting line, does this—and often to
beautiful effect). In other words, he acknowledges the conventional
usage and works from it, thereby establishing a convention in his
own poetry which we are led to take as a general guide. On other
occasions, however, he can effect the same kind of break with, as far
as one can determine, no such intention in mind:

> *There is*
> *the*
> *microscopic*
> *anatomy*
>
> *of*
> *the whale*

Williams can hardly be this bewildered about his whale; his tyrannic,
private measure does the damage. There is a ruinous separation between what Williams conceives to be the 'musical' shape of his
statement and what we can be forgiven for expecting in the way of
dramatic gesture. One could multiply instances where this kind of
indecision seems to operate. That Williams had no real need of such
eccentricities is amply made clear by his 'Asphodel, that Greeny
Flower', the touching poem of love and old age with which the
Pictures from Breughel volume closes. Here there is none of his irritating naughtiness; he takes a longer, more flexible line and only rarely
breaks it against the syntax and cadences of ordinary speech. His
characteristically loose, halting delivery is rigorously shaped by the
painstaking, puzzled emotional commitment which it is the poem's
whole effort to express. If one wishes to talk of the triumph of
Williams's 'colloquial line', the evidence is here; the defeated orthodoxy, though, is that of Experimental Writing. It is perhaps as a
mellow, conciliatory gesture that Williams quotes Spenser's 'Sweet
Thames, run softly . . .' near the end of 'Asphodel'; at any rate he

does it without embarrassment, as if that 'long, dreary, imaginary war' against Europe and the Past were thoroughly forgotten, or irrelevant.

1964

The Forties

I

'It is impossible to indict a whole poetic decade,' wrote Kenneth Allott in 1948, but he was surely wrong. The decade in which he wrote this, the now notorious forties, has been thoroughly written off in most contemporary pigeon-holings. It has popularly become the decade dominated by the punch-drunk Apocalypse, the foaming horsemen, and—as John Wain has diagnosed it—by a wartime hysteria which could only have produced such rubbish:

> If we find much of it impossibly overblown, exaggerated, strained, rhetorical, all we have to do is to remember it was produced under impossible conditions.

This is the routine summary of the period; with war finally declared, we are told, the issues were suddenly private and absolute —in the general chaos it was impossible to maintain not only the clinical admonitory stance, the engaged didacticism of the thirties poets, but also their shapeliness and intelligence. The tortured rhetoric was inevitable, communication just another of the lies. In the words of G. S. Fraser:

> The obscurity of our poetry, its air of something desperately snatched from dream or woven round a chime of words, are the results of disintegration, not in ourselves, but in society.

Encouraged by the example of Dylan Thomas and George Barker, and by the fashionable theory of surrealism, the young poet was confidently able to abandon the knotty, exhausted political struggle and turn instead to Herbert Read's plea for an effort 'to realize some of the dimensions and characteristics of man's submerged being'.

By this, unfortunately, he did not mean what Auden might have meant by such a plea; to the group of poets who banded together in the 1941 anthology, *The White Horseman* (edited by J. F. Hendry and Henry Treece), Freud's main discovery was that it is impossible to talk nonsense. Though claiming to recognize that the subconscious mind is 'a rubbish heap as well as a treasure island', these poets buttressed a neat romantic-classical antithesis with slogans like 'Life just isn't selective', 'Rigorous ruling means unhappiness', 'Order is death', and so on. Against what Hendry maligned as the false objectivism, the pseudo-scientific system-making of the thirties, they proposed a bewildered and permissive Subjectivism (or, as it became, Personalism), a regurgitation of 'significant private myth'. What has come to be regarded as a 'typical forties poem' sprang from this group and goes something like this:

> Crow, wooden lightning, from a sky of thorn—
> O cross-ribbed Adam, tumbled hill of blood.
> While blinded shell and body's thunder churn
> Ear to worm-ball, tongue to lipless stone.
> Our wound is night, bridged in the frigid hours;
> God's manna strung upon a nail spins down
> In skull-tolled bell behind straw eyes, and hoods
> A set dog barking at the rat of heart

The sicklist is a familiar one and there is thankfully no longer any need to dwell on the impenetrable syntax, the glancing evocatives, the Gothic strangulation, the Biblical sequins, etc. The forties threw up hundreds of poems of this kind, and they are really best forgotten. In fact, it is essential that they are forgotten for only then, it seems, will we be able to get at the genuine poetry of the time; in particular, work done during the war years which, in direct descent from Eliot and Auden, attempted to confront the 'disintegration' in personal terms that could make poetic sense out of it.

Keith Douglas, Roy Fuller and Alun Lewis offer three instances of reputations which have suffered from the journalese dismissal of their 'period'. One can think also of certain more minor talents, the

Personal Landscape group, say, and poets like Norman Cameron and Bernard Gutteridge, who have virtually been forgotten. In one or two cases, this neglect may have resulted from the circumstances of publication; poets who wrote out of specific wartime situations publishing in book form well after those situations had been comfortably set aside. Hamish Henderson, for instance, brought out his *Elegies for the Dead in Cyrenaica* and Bernard Gutteridge his *Traveller's Eye* as late as 1948, with the wartime poetry boom long over. In the case of Keith Douglas, who was killed in 1944, there were manuscript problems that delayed the publication of his *Collected Poems* until 1951.

Apart from such factors, though, there has been a general reluctance to investigate the period and a good deal of useful work seems to have been allowed to slip into near-oblivion so that the cliché of the Apocalyptic forties might be maintained. Alun Lewis, for instance, seems to me the most cruelly undervalued poet of the forties and it is interesting to see how a cliché-estimate of him has descended from guide to guide so that it is now, apparently, established as solid ground for ignoring him. The estimate says that Lewis was not really a poet, but a prose writer who had temporarily strayed into verse. It seems to have been originally based on an isolated remark of Lewis's and it first appears in the Penguin *New Writing* obituary notice by Jack Marlowe, where it receives minimal critical support. Since then it has gone into general currency and no longer needs support; one finds it repeated by Stephen Spender, in *Since 1939*, Kenneth Allott in his Penguin *Contemporary Verse*, and Anthony Thwaite in *Contemporary English Poetry*, in almost identical language and with an absolute identity of bald conviction. It might be argued that since Lewis is ignored completely in such general surveys as G. S. Fraser's *Vision and Rhetoric*, and Charles Tomlinson's contribution to the Penguin *Modern Age*, even these insensitivities are something to be grateful for. But this indolent parroting is typical of a total attitude to the period that needs to be called in question.

One wonders, for instance, if the celebrated tact, restraint and common sense of the fifties Movement would have seemed so revolutionary had a more balanced view of their forerunners been current at the time. It is certainly not difficult to trace such qualities in the best war poetry and to find them there upheld in situations where they seem not bleak and faintly preening but heroic and necessary.

'Acceptance seems so spiritless, protest so vain. In between the two I live,' wrote Alun Lewis, and this is a characteristic stance. One finds it echoed in another letter, by Keith Douglas: 'To be sentimental or emotional now is dangerous to oneself and to others. To trust anyone or to admit any hope of a better world is criminally foolish, as foolish as it is to stop working for it. It sounds silly to say work without hope, but it can be done; it's only a form of insurance; it doesn't mean work hopelessly.' To these poets the problem was to give practical meaning to Fraser's glib parenthesis 'not in ourselves'. In Douglas, Fuller and Lewis there is certainly despair at the 'brittle systems', the empires breaking like biscuits, and so on, but what one admires as much as anything else in their work is their determination to be sane in spite of all this. That is to say, to be articulate, and intelligible, a sensitive, fully-functioning participant. Alex Comfort has described his generation as one that 'grew up from early adolescence in the almost complete certainty that we should be killed in action . . . we have all adopted one or another goal—death or refusal.' One might prefer to say that the war poet felt himself to be forcibly adopted by both; a recurrent theme is the threat to his personal identity that is posed by their interpenetration. Depersonalized by the inevitability of death, he is at the same time made acutely aware of his isolation, as an artist, in the practical effort of refusal:

> My photograph already looks historic.
> The promising youthful face, the matelot's collar,
> Say 'this one is remembered for a lyric.
> His place and period—nothing could be duller.'

> Its position is already indicated—

The son or brother in the album; pained
The expression and the garments dated.
His fate so obviously preordained.

The defeated, sardonic manner, the sense of being in an obvious
novel written by someone hardly known and not admired, a slightly
boring cycle that is 'historic' and 'preordained'; these are characteristic of Roy Fuller's *The Middle of a War* (1942; the above is
quoted from its title poem) and *A Lost Season* (1944); one finds
throughout his wartime verse a conflict between on the one hand
'our duties as poets and men', the outside chance that the cycle might
be a creative one, and on the other the natural alienation of the
'slightly inhuman poet', an alienation that can no longer be indulged:

it is goodbye
To the social life which permitted melancholy
And madness in the isolation of its writers.

In 'War Poet', Fuller looks back across literary history and envies
the poets their luxurious idiosyncrasies. For him, the peculiar nightmares are suddenly public and ordinary, the poet wears his matelot's
collar and seems doomed to vacillate between his profound antipathy
to the age, 'the epoch's rage' (apprehended in Fuller with more historical and political self-consciousness than in any other poet of the
time) and his belief in the traditional civilizing responsibilities of the
artist. Beset on the one hand by the suspicion that art, now it is confused with life, can no longer tackle these responsibilities, and that
its integrity is therefore crucially threatened:

Nothing beside the war can be appalling.
The victims of the sacrificial games
Discerned no symbolism in the lions.

and on the other by the fear that he is witnessing an irreparable
corruption of human nature, 'the sudden end of history's thread',
and that:

My living now must bear the laceration

Of the herd, and always will

his most moving and successful poems are nevertheless those in which his identification with 'the herd' is most complete. Service in Africa extended his range of reference, and quickened a descriptive talent which in his earlier volume often seemed vitiated by overt symbolizing and prosaic commentary. The spacious landscapes and the victimized wild animals are, in poems like 'The Giraffes' and 'The Plains', richly projected as metaphors of the communal plight. The immediate dramatic situation needs to be fairly compelling to distract Fuller from Time to 'the very ticking', from the analytic to the straightforwardly metaphoric—he is a reflective writer and too incisively aware of his own ambiguities to be contentedly dramatic. But even so he is at his best when he reflects within experience, at his weakest when he sets up a situation and worries it into generalities. The boredom, the tensions of service life, the leave-takings, the sense of ordinary concerns indefinitely postponed, and so on: familiar situations but Fuller handles them with remarkable reticence. His tone throughout is ironic and compassionate. Later on, he was to look back and see the war as 'something of a bore'. Certainly, such rhetorical modesty had its noble purposes.

One finds a similarly protesting acceptance in Keith Douglas; from his earliest poems he is determined to maintain a 'careful absence of expectation', a 'cynicism' which he is careful to distinguish from apathy. His ambivalent attitude to Oxford, which he sees as at once an idyllic, quaintly pastoral refuge where 'the leisurely immortals dream/venerated and spared by the ominous hours' and a symptom of the general decay of nobility and pleasant scholarship, is firmly underscored by premonitions of certain death:

> *Well, I am thinking this may be my last*
> *summer, but cannot lose even a part*
> *of pleasure in the old-fashioned art of*
> *idleness.*

Like Fuller, he is the resigned audience of his own tragedy; images of acting, dance, jewellery, cosmetics, waxworks, effigies, ghosts, occur time and again—he sees himself as an actor 'waiting in the wings of Europe', Time and Death are 'the villains in the wings'. Of soldiers, he says, 'Think of them as waxworks, or think they're struck/with a dumb immobile spell'; a dead woman's face is 'made up' by death, whose 'quiet hand/Perfects your costume'.

This eye for the statuesque is an aspect also of Douglas's view of himself as the isolated artist, especially burdened by his sensitivity in these unreal conditions. In an early poem, he writes of poets as 'phantoms; boneless, substanceless . . . hated, known to be cursed, guessed to be venomous'. He invents an artist figure of the solitary gardener 'with a swift, sad face and full of phantasy'. In 'Saturday Evening in Jerusalem', he writes of himself:

> Among these Jews, I am the Jew
> the outcast, wandering down the road
> into the hostile dark square.

Persistently, he is 'the solitary person on the lawn' or at the café table from which he perceives his personal isolation to be a cruel intensification of the general predicament:

> I sit at my table and nobody knows
> I've got a beast on my back
>
> *
>
> Our hands meet like strangers in a city
> among the glasses on the table top
>
> *
>
> The noise of people surrounds us
> the sky encloses the whole city
> bending over like a dark theatre
> islanded.

There is very little in Douglas, though, of the sheer documentary impact of reluctant recruits like Fuller and Lewis. Just as at Oxford he had idealized the remote aristocrats of learning, so in wartime he tends to mythologize the chivalric hero, the 'scarlet and tall/ Leisurely fellows' who 'stroll with royal slow motion', a 'gentle/ obsolescent band of heroes'. This attitude somewhat uncomfortably co-exists with an intermittent, and much less convincing, recognition of the physical facts:

> Peter was unfortunately killed by an 88
> it took his leg away, he died in the ambulance
> I saw him crawling on the sand; he said
> It's most unfair, they've shot my foot off

Allowing for their attempt at a Sassoonish ironical terseness, these lines do instance a danger which Douglas did not always escape, that of reticence stiffening into the tightlipped insensitivity of the officers' mess. A poem like 'Vergissmeinicht', which has a powerful plot and is probably Douglas's most famous 'active service' poem, seems finally rather prim and frozen in its formality. It is shoddy in a number of key places—'the paper eye', 'burst stomach like a cave', 'the swart flies', 'the entry of a demon'—and there is a constant, debilitating pressure to make fable: the facts seem wrenched and cerebrally reconsidered; rhyme words clot uncomfortably and there are irritating inversions and compressions. One feels that Douglas might have been happier had the plot been rather less powerful, less limiting to his taste for the spectral.

Douglas is at his best, as I have implied, when he can be remote and speculative, when his verse can enact the unreality of its circumstances and be released by them. Once his early fascination with the skull beneath the skin has tightened into the metaphysical sophistication of 'The Prisoner' and the gay inventiveness of 'Behaviour of Fish in an Egyptian Tea Garden' one feels that he has come close to finding his true voice. Poems like 'Bete Noire' and 'Cairo Jag' mark his limitations just as they predict his likely development, had he lived.

If what one misses in Douglas, finally, is the sense of a firm, discovered personality, there is no such problem with Alun Lewis, the most directly confessional of the important war poets. 'I consider my poems as expressions of personal experience,' he wrote, and again, 'Thinking back on my own writing, it all seemed to mature of a sudden between the winter of 1939 and the following autumn. Can't make it out. Was it Gweno and the Army?' Lewis was called up in 1940, married in 1941; his first book, *Raider's Dawn*, appeared in 1942. It is centrally concerned to 'express at once the passion of love, the coldness of death . . . and the fire that beats against resignation.'

Lewis's stand against the futility of war can often be hysterical and trite; the resonant emblem usually eludes him: 'Nightmare rides upon the headlines', 'blood-soaked forest of disease', 'Mass-rearming for mass-martyrdom', 'mutilated smile', 'wolfish men' and so on, are typical. He is, as he recognized, flabby and invalid when he gets 'too far away from the thing'. But working through particulars of barrack life, leave-taking, life in India, he is most impressive; subtle, exact, rhythmically various, he can allow his general indictment to emerge, climactic and proven, from the actual life it's bred from. He too is self-consciously the artist-soldier, 'sensitive and somehow apart', resentful of his 'crude trade', 'the rough, immediate life of camp',

> the stench
> of breath in crowded tents, the grousing queues,
> And bawdy songs incessantly resung
> And dull relaxing in the dirty bar;
> The difficult tolerance of all that is
> Mere rigid brute routine; the odd
> Sardonic scorn of desolate self-pity,
> The pathetic contempt of the lonely for the crowd.

But what he most passionately resists are the massively dehumanizing temptations of war; and even as he protests he is finally aware that the process has begun, is inexorable, and that he is included. The 'growing self-detachment' is necessary if one is to keep sane (as Lewis develops one senses how his irony becomes a kind of protective skin; his second book is a lot more measured and oblique than

his first and clings more desperately to local detail and sharp parenthesis). For some, this self-detachment engenders self-contempt, a
kind of giggling heroism that is essentially a neurotic trivializing of
the issues; it 'makes men toss their careless lives away' for 'the
honour of the regiment', 'the flashy epaulettes of tradition'; for
others, it can be a means of blurring the responsibility; 'we are the
little men grown huge with death', 'stiff-backed and parrotwise
with pamphlet learning':

> We had certain authority for this
> Not ours, but Another's;
> Our innocence remained with us.

But whatever the motives, in poems like 'The Sentry' and 'Odi et
Amo', Lewis brilliantly enacts the sensation of depersonalized, almost posthumous calm that both protects and reduces the humanity
of the soldier:

> My body does not seem my own
> Now. These hands are not my own
> That touch the hair-spring trigger, nor my eyes
> Fixed on a human target, nor my cheek
> Stroking the rifle butt; my loins
> Are flat and closed like a child's

It is perhaps from such impoverishment that he seeks asylum and
renewal in nature, in its neutrality, and in the images it offers of un-
impeded instinct. The war years produced a great deal of excellent
loco-descriptive verse and one feels that this was not only because
poets were being drafted abroad and confronted with new and ex-
citing places, or because of the general historical and cultural self-
consciousness, though these are clearly factors of importance.
Another impulse—which one finds throughout Lewis—is of retreat
into the permanent, the substantial, the disengaged:

> I sat and watched the dusky berried ridge
> Of yew trees, deepened by oblique dark shafts,

> *Throw back the flame of red and gold and russet*
> *That leapt from beech and ash to birch and chestnut*
> *Along the downward arc of the hill's shoulder,*
> *And sunlight with discerning fingers*
>
> *Softly explore the distant wooded acres,*
> *Touching the farmsteads one by one with lightness*
> *Until it reached the Downs, whose soft green pastures*
> *Went slanting sea and skywards to the limits*
> *Where sight surrenders and the mind alone*
> *Can find the sheeps' tracks and the grazing.*
>
> *And for that moment Life appeared*
> *As gentle as the view I gazed upon.*

In 'Lines on a Tudor Mansion', though, and the excellent 'All Day It Has Rained' it is the immediacy, the transience of natural phenomena that soothes him; the unhistoric instant contrasted approvingly with the 'monumental homes', 'the marble cenotaphs'—this runs throughout also. Finches 'flicker and blossom', 'flash and play'; similarly, the 'dragonflies' blue flicker', 'the soft silk flash of the swifts' are seen as images of the instinctual life that is no longer available to the poet victimized by 'the horror of his century'.

Lewis's poems of separations are among his most memorable, ranging from the lyric intensity of 'Postscript: For Gweno' to the terse despair of 'Goodbye', in which—significantly—much of the exalted vigour of the love poems in *Raider's Dawn* is deliberately frozen into a rhetorical posture. The final stanza represents the out-come of Lewis's struggle against, and for, impersonality:

> *Yet when all's done you'll keep the emerald*
> *I placed upon your finger in the street;*
> *And I will keep the patches that you sewed*
> *On my old battledress tonight, my sweet.*

Just as *Raider's Dawn* is often over-heated into florid exaggeration,

E

so *Ha! Ha! Among the Trumpets* can seem devitalized and prosy; in a sense it is an image of Lewis's personal predicament that this should be so. But totally he knew what was being done to him and what he was losing. Between the two stylistic extremes there is a body of richly balanced verse whose effort is precisely that which distinguishes the significant poetry of the time—the complex but intelligibly managed effort to reconcile the dreamer and the soldier, and be sane.

II

'This is a damned unnatural sort of war,' complained R. N. Currey, and his 'Unseen Fire', though extremely crude, is probably an accurate sketch of the way in which many of the poets of the forties might have responded to the now familiar accusation that their attitude to the war was affectedly unheroic, 'too detached to give any impression of the contact created between the individual and the forces of war and death' and that such an attitude could only produce what Patrick Gardiner denounced as Bore War Poetry.

They might have replied with Currey that the war was a contest between machines and ants; that it was haphazard, fragmentary, and largely an affair of training camps, troopships, Y.M.C.A. hostels and depressing deserts; that it uprooted and despatched but never dignified; that its most tediously insistent threat was to the personal identity which could only be preserved by a sustained effort of sheer accuracy; that it was mechanized, global and usually remote; cheered on by propagandists who had ransacked literature for enticing emblems of nobility and pain, it would finally improve nothing. The anti-rhetorical character of the best war poetry was deliberately a resistance against the propagandist absolutes, the temptation to sag into routine poeticizings over 'the corpse of Europe' or to be terrified into the anonymity of the Apocalypse.

'We do not wish to moralize, only to ease our dusty throats,' wrote Donald Bain in 'War Poet', and this was a typical mood. Ideas were helpless or they were lies, or both—it was now a question of survival and of sanity. Bernard Spencer, for instance, writes of the 'many' whose trust has been 'abused' and, contemplating the 'stubble of conquests', is led to affirm merely the 'minimum wish/for the permanence of the basic things of life', 'the life the generals and the bankers cheat'. Similarly, Hamish Henderson, writing of the war dead, measures their experienced personal loyalties against the rhetoric of sacrifice:

> *What they regretted when they died had nothing to do*
> *with race and leader, realm indivisible*
> *laboured Augustan speeches or vague imperial heritage*
> *(They saw through that guff before the axe fell)*
>   *Their longing turned to*
> *The lost world glimpsed in the memory of letters.*

This view of war as a dreary, pointless and intermittently brutal interruption—and perhaps cancellation—of the personal allegiances that really matter, as a 'cheat' practised by the generals and bankers, as 'guff' disseminated by the propaganda machines and so on, crops up time and again. At worst, the antitheses are too spectacular and the poem will often fade off into cosy nostalgia, a trim domesticated version of Eternal Peace, but at best there is genuine conflict between the active and nostalgic, the responsibility and the dream. This kind of conflict is at the centre of the best modern poetry and, as I have tried to show, to Fuller, Douglas and Lewis the war supplied new terms through which it could be felt.

But the question 'Where are the war poets?' hardly sought this kind of answer. Nor, one imagines, did it aim for the cool ironies of poets like Norman Cameron and Henry Reed, who exploited the neutral stance for sardonic effect. The distinction of tone and texture between, say, Owen's 'Strange Meeting' and Norman Cameron's 'Black Takes White' are usefully representative. Cameron's ironic habit allows him to present the notion 'I am the enemy you killed, my friend' in terms of a comic encounter between two deserting parties, one Negro, the other Italian:

> *The only major movement in those quarters*
> *Was a dense, two-way traffic of deserters.*
>
> *It chanced that a deserting Negro party*
> *Encountered a like-minded Eytie.*
> *At this a keen discussion was engendered*
> *Each party claiming that it had surrendered*
> *And that the other had become its captor.*

The Italians win the argument and the 'embarrassed negroes' are decorated as heroes.

A similarly deflating perception is the excuse for his 'Punishment Enough', which extends compassion to those victims of bombing raids who are caught in shabby underwear. 'It is the petty scale that most appals', he says, but one rather suspects that Cameron could not stop himself reducing things to this level. Cameron is skilful within his narrow limits and unshakeably knowing. He is at his most ambitious when he can deal in archetypes (he is in general overfond of Gravesian wantons and suchlike)—writing of 'the invader' or 'the trigger', his approach will depend on how specific he is trying to be. That is to say, where a real invader will invariably only threaten

> *a desultory shot*
> *Fired more in duty than with aim to kill*

The Invader

> *lives condemned to gorge and crave*
> *To foul his feast with his own hands*
> *At once the oppressor and the slave.*

There are no such uncertainties with Henry Reed, who is altogether a more subtle writer than Cameron. His 'Naming of Parts' and 'Judging Distances' are rightly celebrated as among the best poems written during the war. They set up the familiar opposition between the arid rituals of army training and the full emotional life which is no longer possible, but they do it with enormous skill. The

bees, the flowers, the lovers, the landscape are observed from the
barrack square, nostalgically, and out of the corner of the soldier-
poet's eye. Not only do they mock the manual but—in 'Judging
Distances' where we are told 'how to report on a landscape'—they
are gruesomely included in it. Again it is the depersonalizing threat
of war that has to be confronted. The poet would like to say of
what he sees:

> The still white buildings are like a mirage in the heat
> And under the swaying elms a man and a woman
> Lie gently together.

(and it seems to me that the strength of Reed's 'poetic' lines is often
that they teeter on the edge of embarrassed parody, an enforced dis-
paragement of art in the face of action; but they resist the threat and
move on into a kind of defiant seriousness). The soldier, though,
must have no such language problem. The common denominator
alone can be trusted and the whole of landscape poetry can anyway
be easily reduced to military topography:

> Which is, perhaps, only to say
> That there is a row of houses to the left of arc,
> And that under some poplars a pair of what appear
>   to be humans
> Appear to be loving.

A distance of 'about one year and a half' separates the poet from the
lovers, both literally and as a subject. Similarly the bees who are
'assaulting and fumbling the flowers' are there merely to ridicule
the sexual symbolism of 'opening the breech':

> And this you see is the bolt. The purpose of this
> Is to open the breech, as you see. We can slide it
> Rapidly backwards and forwards; we call this
> Easing the spring.

The bees are, of course, easing the Spring. The pun is managed
without the ruinous smirk one might expect. Indeed, this is what

Reed is really good at—getting the army idiom to work out its own exposure. Drill sergeants habitually pride themselves on never being lost for a sexual analogy and it is from this that much of the irony of 'Naming of Parts' proceeds.

F. T. Prince and Sidney Keyes might appear to be more promising candidates for the full title of War Poet. Prince's 'Soldiers Bathing', for instance, is ambitious enough to be widely regarded as 'perhaps the most noble and memorable poem of the Second World War' (William Plomer) and at first sight it does seem to have a scope and intensity of concern for the suffering combatant which a poet like Reed, for all his fluent sadness, is content not to aim for. Its central image, of a band of soldiers happily washing away the dirt of war, is immediately arresting; but one would have preferred Prince to have dramatized the act more sharply, more mundanely even, than he does, to controlledly feel out its resonance without resorting as he does to parallels from Italian painting. These seem too crudely a strategy for historical depth. The immediate situation is used, really, as a kind of springboard: 'my mind toward the meaning of it strives'. It becomes heaped with routine evocatives of war —'gross', 'rank', 'ravenous', 'disgusting', 'fever', 'filth', 'sweat', 'bestial decay'—and then disappears into speculation, bald analogy and general message-making. Adjectives become automatic: 'soft air', 'frothy tongues', 'terrible pressure', 'pallid flesh'. The argument loosens into obviousness:

> His hatred of war, its terrible pressure
>   that begets
> A machinery of death and slavery,
> Each being a slave and making slaves of others.

and the poet's detachment from the 'soldiers who belong to me', who can be accumulated, by way of a quotation from Lear, into a single emblematic figure and then 'read' as a commentary on 'Michelangelo's cartoon of soldiers bathing', becomes seriously disconcerting.

There is a sudden and significant tightening of the language when

Prince is actually describing the paintings (although 'remember/
muscular/clamber/water/shoulder/eager/slaughter' rather congest
the two-and-a-half lines into which they are packed), particularly
the second one in which:

> warriors, straddled, hacked the foe
> Dug their bare toes into the ground and slew
> The brother-naked man who lay between their feet.

'Dug their bare toes into the ground' is the kind of accurate physical
perception which the poem is generally in need of. One certainly
feels something gets lost when, in stanza four, Prince again founders
into limp generalization. The paintings are now seen as 'indirectly or
directly a commentary/On the Crucifixion'; once again there is the
flood of abstract evocatives and again indecision is suggested by his
persistent refusal to settle for a single word where he can feel
thoroughly insured with two. 'Beneath a sky where even the air
flows/With lacrimae Christi' derives inertly from 'Christ's blood
streaming in the firmament' and it is with relief that one finds the
commonplace meditations on love in stanza five suddenly intensified
into an image of convincingly ferocious power, an image that
renders them redundant:

> The terror of that love has set us spinning in this
> groove
> Greased with our blood.

This same power is felt in the closing lines of 'Soldiers Bathing',
where Prince returns to direct observation of his subjects, who now
'dry themselves and dress':

> Yet, as I drink the dusky air,
> I feel a strange delight that fills me full,
> Strange gratitude, as if evil itself were beautiful
> And kiss the wound in thought, while in the west
> I watch the streak of red that might have issued
>   from Christ's breast.

Here the grandiose-rhetorical impulse really does connect up with the dramatic situation of the poem; for all their melodrama, these lines have sufficient imaginative force and rhythmic vitality to underscore one's main objection to the poem as a whole—that in its pursuit of lofty generalities it persistently loses sight of the experience which these generalities are supposed to spring from. The poem is a noble failure, though, having objectives which very few other of the war poets were prepared to risk.

If, at some level, it is a pious respect for the ambitious, spokesman-like bard that has caused 'Soldiers Bathing' to be overrated, much the same could be said of the reputation of Sidney Keyes. A precocious writer, Keyes was killed after only a fortnight's active service, at the age of twenty. There is little in his work that treats directly of wartime experience although, as with Keith Douglas, the threat always seems to be there. 'I am in love with the rhythm of dead limbs,' Keyes wrote, but his obsession with death never composes into an interestingly deep-felt attitude; he rather toys with the idea of it, as he toys with the idea of war. At times it is as an isolated poet, a plowman without a home, that he cultivates death as 'cold security' from—as he says in a poem to John Clare—'time's contempt for such as you and I' or, more specifically, from his own contemporary situation. His 'Elegy for Virginia Woolf' is in this vein:

> Lie low, sleep well, safe from the rabid winds
> Of war and argument, our hierarchies and powers.

It is 'easy, easy as sleep', it seems, and Keyes's affectation of premature old age accompanies this view of himself as 'the lost traveller frozen in the field'. He refers to his 'old hand writing in frost', 'the cold eye and the failing hand' and resents that 'Time will not grant . . . the hand respite'. There is something rather too neatly fanciful in his easy distribution of wintry euphemism, and the archaic cast of his vocabulary helps to persuade that his attraction to death was more to an adolescent style than a genuine despair.

Death is not always courted, though, and often Keyes discovers an active nobility in his role as elegist and spokesman:

> *Fear paralysed all striving; shook the strong*
> *And broke the weak, only could never*
> *Subdue the writing hand, none may subdue the hand.*

It is in this spirit that he confronts the 'invader' who will be 'stealing our dreams or breaking up/Our history for firewood' and consoles the victims:

> *Let them take what they want, even our dreams,*
> *Somewhere our loss will plant a better orchard.*

He writes of the 'incredible spring' that awaits the 'triumph of clear decision' and is easily tempted into the hortatory:

> *go on, go out*
> *Into the bad lands of battle, into the cloud wall*
> *Of the future, my friends, and leave your fear*

or, worse still:

> *O live and love to see your happy children*
> *Deny the sorrow of a burning world*

The 'lion-hearted poet' can contribute to this effort. Now and then, the attitudinizing breaks down and there can be a touching direct-ness and incompetence:

> *But I am frightened after every good day*
> *That all my life must change and fall away.*

Writing of himself as a 'War Poet', he says 'I am the man who groped for words and found/An arrow in my hand'. It seems typical of Keyes that it should be an arrow and not, say, a Bren gun. He finds it as impossible to treat of the materials, the concrete situations of modern warfare as he does to 'sing' with what he calls 'the foul tongue of a soldier'; it is usually 'the soldier's drum', 'the horse-hair plume' or, at best, 'brass and iron'.

Sidney Keyes never got significantly beyond Poetic Diction. The very facility and imitative skill which one finds remarkable in a

writer of his age must surely have inhibited his effort for a personal
voice. It is perhaps unfair to complain that he wrote unconvincingly
about a war in which he took so brief an active part (it is believed
that there were active service poems, written in Africa, but no trace
of them has been found); at the same time, though, it is as a war poet
that Keyes is applauded in critical studies that have no mention of,
say, Alun Lewis and it is in these terms that his achievement must be
questioned.

III

In his introduction to *Eight Oxford Poets*, Sidney Keyes claims a common romanticism for the poets he selects and apologizes for what he
calls their 'tendency to over-floridity'. The reason is, he implies,
'that we have on the whole little sympathy with the Audenian
school of poets'. This crude antithesis might have been a useful one
for Keyes himself, as it was for the contributors to *The White Horseman*, but it hardly serves to describe the work of, say, Keith Douglas
and it badly misrepresents the other really interesting poet in Keyes's
anthology, Drummond Allison. Allison was killed in action and left
one posthumous volume of verse, *The Yellow Night*—it is uneven,
idiosyncratic and full of undergraduate vanities, but there is much in
it that ought not to be forgotten.

Allison was perhaps the most absorbed and striking elegist of
Auden's 'low, dishonest decade'. As with Roy Fuller, his problem
was to maintain a real political involvement in spite of the discredited
systems, the expiring hopes of the thirties, and to properly inherit
the Auden manner while at the same time registering his private
despair that the conditions which energized it no longer prevailed.
His debts to Auden are obvious and considerable—his alliteration,
his telegraphese, his menacing inventories, his quirky, observant
symptomatizing—but essentially he is fascinated by an attitude
which he understands to have failed. It is in his treatment of the
difficulties that arise from this that his real interest lies.

'What never waxed has waned' is the lament that insistently threatens Allison's brusque, nostalgic tour of the old middle-class targets, his borrowed eye for the 'concave chest', the 'love-sick seizure', the 'impure dreams'. The heroes have returned from their chivalric quest and have resigned themselves to a 'prehistoric fear', the continuity of evil as confirmed by literature and legend. Very often Allison's disenchantments have an automatic ring:

> No remedy, my retrospective friend,
> We've found no remedy;
> Nor from these fields the briared and barbed wire edge
> Can keep our enemy,
> To mend the gaps
> Would take perhaps a century.

Such pious gloom hardly suits him, though; he is at his best when he can observe or invent. But where Auden can list and document with racy confidence, Allison can merely fumble with his acutely spotted 'toastrack mouth', 'blackcurrant pastilled breath' and so on—the details don't add up, the admonitory motive that might have cohered them has gone hollow:

> For roads and poems, food and fabled animals
> Hands, films and singing, sunlight cutting clouds
> We cannot love completely if we lack
> An attitude.

'Make me see/Shapes are related', Allison exclaims at one point, but in all his intermittently brilliant documentary verse there is this central discomfiture, the missing 'attitude', and it seems to worry his language to curious extremes—on the one hand an almost impenetrable compression which is at least energetic and peculiar, and on the other a self-explanatory slackness which is at best honest and sad. So easily do his instances slip out of range of his ideas that he often seems unable to decide whether he is being allegorical or realistic. Predictably enough, his best poems are his most literary and artificial: 'After Lyonesse', for instance, seems to aim at an inclusive emblem of the thirties enterprise—the Serf, 'louseclothed scabskinned swartsouled', considers the defeated heroes, their 'effeminate pale bangles', their 'brooches at belt' and sardonically reduces their cloudy endeavour to the 'cold truth' of mean ambition. 'They are thin literature, I am life', he concludes

> *They were the haughty surface, now my knife*
> *Probing beneath proves their self-conscious strife*
> *Dramatisation of a theme as ancient*
> *As Merlin's nameless father.*

Allison tries to prove the same thing himself in 'We Shall Have Company'. It is not clear if the Serf in 'After Lyonesse' is supposed to have been deceived by his political or his cultural leaders, but at one level certainly the distance between the 'pale bangle' and the 'louse-cloth' measures the effectiveness of political verse. Thus, in 'We Shall Have Company', it is the shop steward who threatens 'every watchful author' and the poet's fear is that 'soon our class/Is to be flung through doors it opened with such care'. Should this happen, the poet will join forces—not with Arthur this time, but with the prehistoric monsters. It is significant that when Allison lists the seamen, the colonists, the clerks in the suburbs, the miners, the centre-forwards and the 'clergy proud of God their son' and predicts their destruction, he makes explicit that delight in the variety of a class-ridden social scene which is at the back of Auden's most malevolent roll-calls. It is not surprising that he should envisage for himself a truly thirty-ish doom and 'go down'

> *Like one too late*
> *Discovering the examiners were serious*

Even so, he seems to say, answering them can surely still be fun. Believing this, Allison is at his most assured:

> *We shall ride out on quaggers, on mastodon and mammoth,*
> *Pat old triceratops in passing, stroke the dinosaur.*
> *Sung to pterodactyls we shall strew*

Food for roc, the great auk and the moa.
Giant sloth and sabre-tooth shall grow tame for us.
Neanderthal and Piltdown will be willing guides to us
And ichthyosaurus wallow no longer malevolent.

(Incidentally, if this sounds like something by Ted Hughes, it is worth looking out Allison's 'Yorktown Gate Guard' for some early Thom Gunn.) In his poems from Sandhurst and the Battle School, the military metaphor is employed rather naughtily and with a literary bravado to encompass the doom of personal relationships ('the minefields of my fear', 'only Death/Can quash this constitution and subject us both', etc.) and Allison sets off for war with a dubious aplomb: 'I'll make eastward haste for eager Dover.' One wonders how this strange, uncertain talent might have developed under stress of the real thing. A familiar speculation, but with Allison one feels its pointlessness to be unusually exasperating.

It is clear, though, that the Audenesque eye could not roam across a battlefield, or an Indian bazaar, with anything like the panache that enlivens its English views. Part of the fun and the expertise was in revealing, or pretending, that the English prewar scene *was* a battlefield. The range could be as diverse and eccentric as the poet pleased and he could always feel confident with his peculiar diagnostic skills—he was spotting what would not otherwise be spotted, he was worrying a habitual landscape into alarming, uniquely discerned appearances. There was room, in other words, for imagination and vanity; a rare chance to combine extreme idiosyncrasy with genuine political concern. Now given the real thing, the burden of obvious suffering, the manner is likely to go limp. The specialist role is lost and in the face of actual calamity it is impossible to be dotty or, even, very clever.

One can either be personal, direct and intensely concentrated as, say, Alun Lewis was (though he was never Audenesque to start with) or Roy Fuller, in their best work, or one can eliminate the personality from one's reportage and merely document. A useful instance of this common direction is offered by Bernard Gutteridge.

Gutteridge survived the war but has only brought out one volume, *The Traveller's Eye*, which, like Allison's, is hard to get hold of. In his early poems, Gutteridge can confidently play what he calls 'an imagist's game' and inject a generalized menace into his lively descriptions of severe English landscapes, shooting parties, fêtes, and so on. His similes are industriously modish without really coming off ('blood/Flecking like shredded petals of geranium', 'its velvet green neckband like a spinster/Twisted') and he often tails off into cumbersome explication of his own analogies. For instance, in a poem about shooting a hare, it will be pointed out

> *And that is how—deliberately aiming,*
> *Cold pressure of the trigger—you have destroyed*
> *My leaping heart.*

But he has some striking crystallizations ('the doctor's shadow on the blind') and on the whole his scrupulous observation does project a small, threatened world which he can control and be clever with.

In Burma, though, confronted with the 'shuffling, bombed, shelled and outlawed peasants', his language loses its decisive edge, his 'imagist's game' becomes 'these arid lines' and he is forced back into a desperate piling up of adjectives, into a kind of selfless precision which cramps and nullifies his early vigour: 'slant-eyed, untrustworthy Burmans', 'drabbish, flatchested women', 'hoary sly old men', 'flash, slick dirty youths'—the catalogue is endless, well-meant but finally routine. But to break out of it is for him to have 'our bullets yelping after like harriers/Keen on a kill' or to compare parachutists with puppets:

> *Only five puppets entire among twisted and shattered bodies*
> *They hint with their crooked jumps at the string's wangling*
> *As they once more jerk into a mockery of the fascinated evenings*
> *Before the nursery burned.*

'In the presence of the violent reality of war, consciousness takes the place of the imagination,' Wallace Stevens has written, and a number of the war poets found themselves caught guiltily and ineffectually between the two. In Bernard Spencer, for instance, the conflict is explicit; his personal situation—that of a civilian exile in Cairo—might have helped to sharpen the antithesis. Living on 'this ground of peace', he is able to see himself as 'the shadow of the shadow of war', and to keep a direct hold on what the war threatened to destroy. Much as Allison returned to suburbia, so Spencer sees ordinary life persisting in Salonica (with the difference that to Spencer what he sees is 'a holiday photo' and he can wonder of it: 'What difference if I wish good luck to these foreigners, my hosts?'):

> The dancing, the bathing, the order of the market, and as day
> Cools into night, boys playing in the square;
> Island boats and lemon-peel tang and the timeless café crowd
> And the outcry of dice on wood.

'I would shut the whole if I could out of harm's way', he concludes, but is forced to acknowledge that there no longer 'exists a word or a lock which gunfire may not break/Or a love whose range it may not take'. This is a recurrent pattern, keeping love out of range: 'To write good poetry [a modern poet] has to brutalize himself back out his upbringing. His dangers are that, faced with injustice, violence and squalor, he may either get numb, frigid, over-intellectual or soft, sentimental,' Spencer wrote, and his verse ranges uneasily between these two extremes. On the one hand, there is the defiant aestheticism of 'Death of an Airman' and on the other the solemn prosiness of 'Base Town', a poem which shows that Auden's lessons are not easily unlearned:

> And the lie,
> The twist of reason,
> The clever rumour planted in the nerves,
> The dossier infecting like a sinus.

It is the yachts, the dancers, the 'full-rigged ship', images of lucidity and graceful composure, which really attract Spencer and one feels that he would prefer not to nag at them, that the war was just remote enough for him to feel impatient with what it was demanding

of him as a poet. The closing of 'A Cold Night' puts it baldly, but
usefully:

> And one needs time to sit in peace
> Opposite one's girl, with food, fire, light,
> And do the work one's own blood heats,
> Or talk, and forget about the winter
> —This season, this century—and not be always
> Opening one's doors on the pitiful streets
>
> Of Europe, not always think of winter, winter, like
>   a hammering rhyme
> For then everything is drowned by the rising wind, everything
>   is done against Time.

IV

'The subject is too large and looms too near; it crushes the writer.
All we can do is provide footnotes, the small detailed cameos of our
experience'; this feeling of Gavin Ewart's was shared by a number
of his contemporaries in war-time and for a few of them it meant
release into mild ironies. For Ewart himself, certainly, it meant that
he could exclaim over the Bofors AA Gun: 'Such marvellous ways
to kill a man . . . the well-oiled shining marvel of our day.' I have
already tried to show that it was perhaps just this kind of misgiving
that encouraged the anti-rhetorical virtues which characterize the
really interesting poetry of the period. In the very best of Lewis,
Douglas and Fuller, for instance, one does not feel personal experience to be of mere footnote value but rather to provide the only
vital terms in which so general and so variously detailed a catastrophe could be written about.

At the same time, though, it is evident that throughout even the
more durable work of the period there is a persistent and often disruptive effort after the finally inclusive emblem, a nostalgia almost

for a situation like that of the First World War (Ewart, for instance, makes the point that 'the best poems about modern war have already been written . . . most of them by Wilfred Owen'), where the poet could confidently assume an admonitory or spokesman-like role, make articulate the afflictions of his generation and know, as Owen did, that 'All a poet can do today is warn.'

Owen, of course, could envisage an audience that needed to be stirred into a realization of what war was really about, an audience either innocent or complacent, and one well-used to being lulled by the kind of volunteer patriotics which the Conscription Act had made not only impossible but unnecessary to entice from the poet of World War II. According to Robert Graves, it was through 'a mist the colour of khaki blanco' that the mechanized conscript recalled 'the amateur, desperate, happy-go-lucky, ragtime, lousy army of World War I'. The isolation that the World War I poet felt from his audience tended to be expressed in World War II as the isolation that the poet-soldier felt from his fellow soldiers—his civilian audience, very often, was having a worse time than he was. 'While so many soldiers had no better activity than cleaning buttons, drilling and parading, etc. . . . their wives and children were at the mercy of enemy bombers in the towns,' wrote John Waller, and although Graves surely exaggerated when he went on to say that 'the soldier has, on the whole, lived a far safer life than the munition-maker whom, in World War I, he despised as a shirker', it was clearly true that there were few grounds for believing that the poet's function was to warn, awaken or inform.

It is interesting that not only did the loss of this function help to devitalize the Auden manner (as I tried to suggest in the third section of this essay), it also undermined the ambitions of the New Apocalypse. In Oscar Williams's anthology, *The War Poets*, there is a curious contribution from Henry Treece. It amounts, really, to an obituary of the movement which Treece had helped to found. The poet's role before the war, he maintains, had been to predict 'ultimate disintegration'—'My poetry, that is, had *known* that all this would happen and had prepared itself for the chaos.' He had joined

F

the R.A.F., he says, as a *man*, so that he would not feel ashamed of himself 'as the years went on', but as a *poet* he was 'naturally cynical of such behaviour'. He had found, since joining up, that he had been able to keep up a steady supply of verse for a short time on the strength of what remained of his 'pre-war craftsman's energy' but now that the catastrophe which he had been predicting had in fact happened all he wanted now was to become 'a quiet, private person again'.

At this point in the argument it is no longer clear if Treece is talking as man or as poet—as man, presumably, since he found that he was now no longer able to write poetry. But he pulls himself together and goes on to insist that, despite everything, 'the poet's function is to seek out the germ of all war, to isolate and parade it as a warning against future disease of this sort . . . to prevent such horror for the future'. Beneath the pomposity, there is a characteristic desperation that refuses, in effect, to abdicate from one of the most cherished poetic roles, that will not yield a theoretical inch from the central 'prophetic' station. The kind of meaningless exclusiveness that forces a separation between *poet* and *man* is, in the circumstances of service life, absolutely necessary to a writer of Treecian pretensions, and the refusal to confront the predicted catastrophe in reality, in terms of its specific human occasions, is exactly what one would expect from a school of poetry that subsists on its assumptions of omniscience. The Apocalyptic cant about 'the necessity for the individual to control the political and philosophical Machine' ought to have discovered, in wartime, a peculiar opportunity for relevance; it is, though, precisely in these mechanized, dehumanizing circumstances, that the movement is revealed to have been a mere flourishing of godheads. Deprived of his unknowing flock, and of the glamour of prophesy, the poet steps down and becomes, reluctantly, a man.

The best that could be hoped for by the Apocalyptics was either Treece's audience of the future, a fairly slight ideal as things stood, or the possibilities of the representative lament. Chaos having arrived, the priestly bard would still bemoan it on behalf of a flock no longer unknowing but at least inarticulate and anxious to be spoken for. A poem like David Gascoyne's 'Miserere' is typical of this genre, demanding as it does 'Is man's destructive lust insatiable?' Popular Christian symbolism provides a framework within which the poet can sicken freely: 'bitter truth', 'spattered blood', 'putrid flesh', 'cold eyes, unsmiling lips', 'guilty stains'—none of these clichés having any particular reference—can be dispensed with a blind amplitude. Now and then, of course, tiny glimmers of hope can be allowed to infiltrate:

> Man's long journey through the night
> may not have been in vain

The tone is almost single-pitched, the plaintive here and there accelerating into the frantic, or braking violently into the dutifully biblical. Where reality is permitted to intrude, it merely rattles the props:

> Draw now with prickling hand the curtain back;
> Unpin the black-out cloth; let in
> Grim crack-of-dawn's first glimmer through the glass.

If Gascoyne's pretence is of shedding everyone's tears, this is somehow less irritating than Vernon Watkins's harnessing of the same generalized emotions to specific public figures. His much-anthologized poem on the death of Werfel is actively offensive in its hollow speculative gestures:

> O God, the atom has split in Werfel's brain.
> The room is rigid with the death of his brain.
> O small, diminished wall of their jealous fury
> Propping the chaste stars of his huge horizons.

In the many, similarly unfelt post-mortem poems that appeared during the war, the prophetic role is seen to have found a new lease of life. If the poet could no longer forecast the Flood, he could still draw back the veil for its victims. Watkins, in particular, is often discovered at the centre of his verse in some quasi-divine posture:

> *I summon serene typhoons,*
> *Earthquakes, storms of sand,*
> *Glaciers calving like moons.*

This is a typical boast. In its service, dead sailors get buried beneath Watkins's version of them as 'magnificent types of godhead' who are, after death, seen busily accusing the 'sea-god'. And in George Barker's meditations on the same subject, the sailors are even more objectionably portrayed as swimming 'through green eternity'. One feels that it is no whimsical hypothesis when Barker asks:

> *Was I the shape of Jesus*
> *When to me hopeward their eyeballs swivelled?*

It is certainly with true Messianic conviction that Barker kindly addresses himself to the distressed lovers, widows and children and assures them that they are 'awaiting change they cannot understand'.

Excesses of this kind and the grandiose assumptions that lie behind them are typical of a considerable body of World War II poetry and they are rather too well-remembered already. It should be emphasized, however, that although very few poems of the period succeeded in the kind of generalizing wisdom which Barker and Watkins so brashly assume, the objective of an inclusively 'representative' war poetry was not always pursued in this way. In a number of cases it distracted more honest poets from their real gifts and imposed on them an unmanageable ambition.

What is valuable, for instance, in Alan Ross's *The Derelict Day* are the moments in which the desolation of occupied Germany, the 'deadness, apathy and self-pity', is allowed to infiltrate modestly direct description. Ross's strength is that he can visualize fairly complex landscapes, natural settings and so on, without getting too bogged down in prosy detail. The best poems in the book are those in which he does this and at the same time manages to say things about the general defeat, of both victor and victim. One senses, though, throughout the volume, an effort to push beyond such limits, to judge and define in more overt, discursive terms, and where this is attempted it invariably seems to deaden Ross's language into a rather facile reliance on key words like 'empty', 'hopeless', 'diseased' or into slack generalizations about 'the human world's defeat'. This is a pity because the point about the refugees, prisoners and exiles who populate this book is that they labour under a common paralysis of spirit, and it seems altogether appropriate for the poet to register his response to this with a kind of bare, dazed particularity. He too is afflicted and not able finally to judge, prophesy or console:

> *The blown bridge leans towards the dykes, one end*
> *suspended in a hand floating on the dirty scum*
> *of water. A green tunic huddles like a trodden cloth;*
> *nearby, two wrists grope beneath a petrol drum.*
>
> *Pinned on mud walls are photos of naked girls:*
> *A bloodstained map is marked with useless lines.*
> *Two liqueur glasses standed wedged between the sights,*
> *and, planted like flowers, beneath the gun, are glass mines.*

In a similar way, one feels of a poet like Julian Symons that he is a good deal less impressive when he is denouncing the 'apathy of a decaying Empire', 'greed of the American paw' and

> *the murderers,*
> *the corrupt class, the scum*
> *of a top-heavy civilisation*

than when he is following his own 'first rule: observe'. Symons is probably the nearest to a Sassoon that the Second World War produced, in the sense that he wrote more angrily about the political ends of the war, 'the second capitalist war', than anyone else did. But it is an anger which is perpetually persuading him into the looseness of prose polemic:

> *Note; the nationalist murderers in terms of the*
> *wonderfully benevolent Europe of the future.*

The indignant stance is difficult to maintain, and there is very little that is tightly caustic or subtly barbed in Symons's complaints. One feels that he is more at home when he is wavering between 'the private virtue and the public good' or, better still, when he will allow that 'the moment exists and is real' without immediately having to founder into, 'What is reality? Do not ask that.' When Symons allows his hospital ward a dramatic rather than a symptomatic presence he can be impressively sensitive:

> It is quiet
> In the ward; sunlight on the wooden floor
> Floods; there are flowers and ferns in bowls.
> The wind blows through
> The window beside me, fresh and cool.

*   *   *

It ought to be said, I think, as a footnote to this essay that the point has not been to provide an inclusive account of English poetry 1940–50. Any such account would have to include a number of poets whom I have not mentioned. My first assumption was that the term 'forties poet' is currently one of easy critical abuse. It is usually taken to refer to the New Apocalypse writers and their descendants, whose badness is usually accounted for in terms of 'war-time hysteria'. It seems to me that any talk about the forties as a literary period ought to begin with a more accurate definition of the verse directly occasioned by the war, and it is this, simply, that I have tried to supply.

1964

Roy Fuller

The title of Roy Fuller's *Buff* derives from the following snatch of dialogue, quoted from an old Forfeits Game:

> *'Methinks Buff smiles'*
> *'Buff neither laughs nor smiles'*

and it seems to embody what has always been a familiar warning, or misgiving, in Fuller's work; that we should not be misled into assuming that the poet has anything like the coolly authoritative command of experience that his elegant forms, his trim vocabulary, his wittily self-effacing parentheses, and so on, might seem to imply. Indeed, it is perhaps Buff's real distress that his expressions should so readily invite this sort of misinterpretation, that the style he has to be content with is as insufficiently nourished by direct feeling as the personality, or state of mind, he wants it to express.

Although Fuller has admitted before that the 'prim ego's guesses' are unlikely to encompass the 'cesses of the Id', that the rational, discursive manner cannot receive the full weight of imaginative experience and do very much with it except perhaps shrivel its mystery into a few punily inexact, if clever, propositions, he has nevertheless invariably preferred to rely on the certainties of what he calls an 'austere miss' rather than on the possibilities of a 'romantic woolly hit'. Few poets, though, can so often publicly have found their own work to be as 'boring' as Fuller seems to find his; time and again he has turned on what he has done and scoffingly dismissed it as inadequate to the real demands of the age, as pitifully falling short of what he sees as the traditional civilizing responsibilities of art:

> *I do not know which are the most obscene;*
> *Poets, profoundly sceptic, scared, unread;*

> *The leaders monolithic in their mania;*
> *Or the unteachable mass as good as dead.*

A child of the thirties, Fuller was not able to turn in his political dis-
illusion to the contemplation of any 'staggering equation/or mystic
experience'; all systems failed and his unsatisfactory refuge, always
guiltily inhabited, has been precisely that life of the imagination
which he has continued to wish might be shared by the oppressed
and barbarous 'common fold'. The separation between his rarefied
personal life and those regrettable 'ordinary modes of being' which
he is yet committed to, has become wider with age so that now—
and this kind of honesty runs painfully throughout *Buff*—more than
ever is it difficult to decide who is the more to be pitied, who is the
more tragically deprived; the poet, neurotically withdrawn, beset
by nightmares, symbols and impossible cravings, or his lost audience,
philistine, exploited, briefly instinctual.

Fuller has never quite yielded up such moral questions in despair,
to devote himself to, say, the devout recreation of those fabulous,
legendary, effective qualities of action which he so often mourns
('fabulous', 'legendary', 'marvellous', 'incredible'—the adjectives
keep cropping up but rarely are these ideals given much dramatic
conviction; they are invoked, discussed, glanced at longingly, but
are persistently in tension—argued rather than felt—with the poet's
duties to the 'cheap, scarred times' that have no place for them); the
tough, responsible, empirical obligations of the rational intelligence
cannot allow the poet to pretend that he actually is—even in some
private dreamland—a 'captain' or a 'martyr':

> *How different from the captain and the martyr*
> *Is he who walks, this rainy afternoon,*
> *The streets of monuments deformed by time,*
> *Stopping at photographs of girls with flowers*
> *For nipples and with thighs beyond his powers*
> *Racking his memory for a useless rhyme.*

In some way, perhaps, it is just this refusal to 'dissemble', to pretend that he is not bound to the 'unteachable mass', if only by lust, envy or the shrinking, pointless ambition to translate dream into reality, that gives Fuller's style what often seems to be its almost temporary quality; he obeys the rules but there is always this suspicion that he feels not only rhyme but all the taxing stanzaic patterns he sets himself to be 'useless', in the sense that they have no central expressive or synthesizing function in the modern world. In the absence of any convincing alternative, the 'noble tune' which he often seems to be hoping someone else will come up with, he will continue to employ them scrupulously—the incongruity between despairing subject and impassive form can, after all, perhaps mirror the division in the poet's own nature between the fabulous pursuits of his imagination and the neutral, playing safe, persona that he offers to the world. The weary scepticism that informs Fuller's 'Once more the meditative poem . . .' is, it seems to me, also somewhere present in his continued reliance on the merely available technique: 'Once more the sonnet sequence', 'Once more the villanelle' are other conceivable opening lines. This is, of course, one way of coming to terms with the technical impasse which other modern poets, less seriously disposed to worry over their historic role, have had crazily experimental answers to, and there is a glum, impressive kind of dignity to it.

It might be wishful, or at least arrogant, thinking to suggest that this is in any sense Fuller's own conscious attitude to his technique, but in a work like, say, the sequence *To X*, where a number of oddities and circumlocutions are encouraged by his scheme of sharing out two rhyme-sounds per individual poem, the cumulative effect is of there being a considerable (ironic? we ask hopefully) distance between the very painful and genuinely felt subject of the poem (the poet this time imagining himself to be involved in a clandestine love affair and exploring the art/life antitheses that arise out of the attempt) and the somewhat pedantic engineering that encases it. Looked at in terms of sheer ingenuity it is all enormously well done but rhymes like 'groin/quoin/macedoine' or recurrent awkwardnesses like

> *On long green legs, in something thick and grey*
> *That to your youthful bust was not quite thwarting*

and

> *but time had failed to parallel*
> *My love with any stuff that could cohere*

and

> *Remarks you uttered were extremely few*
> *That shed on the murk between us any light*

tend to suggest that the 'old played out poet' who is the work's protagonist is being dramatically credited with the sort of technical diffidence that we are implicitly advised to expect from him. Alarmed and gratified to find himself 'still capable of pain' he yet chooses to throttle his pain with a too composed self-mockery, with too blatantly literary gestures. That he should do this is also painful to him, one guesses, but if it is there is no way that he can explore it:

> *to have longed in vain*
> *when a mere sentence might have let me fold*
> *In scrawny arms your vigorous white and gold.*

There is a kind of afterthought defensiveness about this last line (the cartoon 'scrawny', the literary 'white and gold') and it is not enough to argue that, though terrible, the predicament expressed here is also slightly comic. It is appropriate, in character, that the hero should fear being caught with his trousers down but to have him this fully clothed throughout the whole poem seems rather to be taking advantage of him.

The hero of *Buff*'s closing sequence, 'The Historian', is similarly buried beneath the weight of his own self-consciousness. In his declining years, he chronicles the collapse of cultivated, spectacular empire, finding in its relics a retreat from the doomed world of the 'infected mass'. The barbarians are the more dreadful as his own barbarous energies diminish, his historical and political truths are seen to be sorely relative. To what extent, for instance, is his resistance to change simply the envy of old age:

> *age's censure of the lascivious*
> *To which it is by appetite impelled*
> *In vain—its horror of a licence which*
> *Its earlier tolerance handed to its daughters.*

As with the sequence *To X* there is in this work—and indeed in the
book as a whole—a degree of wisdom and honest self-analysis that is
rare and useful in contemporary poetry. Fuller's intelligent readiness
to think out his relations with the traditionally major concerns of
poetry is consistently brave and admirable. To nag at him to be more
lyrically direct, more richly metaphoric, more free and natural in his
speech is simply to repeat what he has already said himself. Of his
rhymes, for instance, he can disarm with lines like

> *A middle-aged suburban fountain pen*
> *That rhymes carcinogen with magdalen.*

Of his tendency to regard the external, visual world as explicitly
symptomatic and to remorselessly argue out the significance of his
direct perceptions, he is ready to concede that

> *I stop my car to let a girl*
> *Carrying a dog, cross the road;*
> *And think 'Girl with a Dog', but wonder*
> *If in fact art is better than life*

As long as Fuller is as shrewdly aware of what he is up to as he un-
doubtedly is in *Buff*, then we in turn in least concede that his austere
hits *are* infinitely preferable to a lot of other people's woolly
romantic misses.

1965

Robert Lowell

1. *Lord Weary* to *Life Studies*

The title of Robert Lowell's first large-scale collection, *Lord Weary's Castle*, was cleverly chosen. The ballad of Lambkin tells how Lord Weary hired a mason to build him a castle and, when the job was done, refused to pay him for it. The mason took his revenge by breaking into the castle and murdering Lord Weary's wife and child. Ingratitude, exploitation, the indefensible failure of obligation to God that man is guilty of and must be violently punished for; these are pervasively the concerns of Lowell's early verse.

A Bostonian turned Catholic, it is with some relish that Lowell imagines the torments of hell prefigured in terms of the locale whose traditions he is out to revile; there is a sense in which he sees himself as the nurse who let the wronged mason into Lord Weary's Castle. Lowell's Catholicism has been well described as simply a way of abusing Calvinism and in his most consciously scathing assaults on fallen Boston it does fall into an extrinsic role, becomes not much more than a convenient and rather decorative position to attack from. It is no cure for the ills it helps to diagnose.

Like Jonathan Edwards, whose biography Lowell once started to write and on whose works some poems are explicitly based, he can make 'chimneys suddenly leap into flame in the midst of a revival meeting'. Boston is part of hell

> *disgrace*
> *Elbows about our windows in this planned*
> *Babel of Boston where our money talks*
> *And multiplies the darkness . . .*

its streets are 'hell-fire streets', its adulterers grow scales like the

serpent in Eden, its waters are 'fouled with the blue sailors', victims
not only of war, but also of Quaker profiteering. It is that 'lack of
common consistency' which Melville found in the Quaker Captain
Peleg that is the subject of Lowell's central early poem, *The Quaker
Graveyard in Nantucket*, ostensibly an elegy for a dead relative, but
more deeply a bitter appraisal of New England morality:

> Though refusing, from conscientious scruples, to bear arms
> against land invaders, yet himself had illimitably invaded
> the Atlantic and Pacific; and though a sworn foe to human
> bloodshed, yet had he in his straight-bodied coat, spilled
> tuns upon tuns of leviathan gore . . . very probably he had
> long since some to the sage and sensible conclusion that a
> man's religion is one thing, and this practical world quite
> another. This world pays dividends.

By relating Ahab's whaleboats to the North Atlantic Fleet (Lowell
was a conscientious objector to World War II) he is as much concerned
to express his hatred of war as of a hypocritical pacifism, but if one
recalls the tablets on the walls of the whaleman's Chapel in *Moby
Dick*, and Melville's description of the Nantucketers as 'like so many
Alexanders', who have 'overrun and conquered the watery world',
there can be little doubt as to where the emphasis lies. Nor can there
be any mistaking the manner; it is substantially that of Father
Mapple who, 'when describing Jonah's sea-storm, seemed tossed by
a storm himself' and who, although enjoying a 'wide reputation for
sincerity and sanctity' is yet open to suspicion of 'courting notoriety
by . . . mere tricks of the stage'.

Grotesqueries are frequent in these early poems—in one, a dead
ancestor of Lowell's is met by a Christ who walks across the water
of Boston's public gardens to take him 'beyond Charles River to the
Acheron'; in another, the Virgin's 'scorched, blue thunderbreasts of
love' are asked to 'pour buckets of blessings on my burning head'.
Lowell's puns ('torn-up tilestones crown the victor') come from the
same malignant source and they are so recognizably part of his
manner tha when one encounters, in *Poems 1938–49*, what is prob-

ably a misprint—a reference to a corpse's 'heel-bent deity' (it's 'hell-bent' in the American edition)—one cannot be entirely sure, since a few lines back there are some 'heel-headed dogfish', that a pun is not intended. This is not as trivial as it might sound. Lowell is a clotted and extremely difficult writer in these early poems—there are whole passages which seem to make no sense at all—and if one is to work at him one needs some guarantee that he is not prone to mere ingenuities. (For example, is there a meaningful relation between the 'heavy lids' of the sea-gulls in *The Quaker Graveyard in Nantucket* and the 'heavy eye-lids' of Our Lady of Walsingham in the same poem? There could be, of course, but what matters is that a signalled relation is not developed beyond that point where the author might justifiably be suspected of either slovenliness or casual dexterity.)

Lowell's obscurity too rarely seems to be founded on long hard effort to be understood. It arises most often where his subject is explicitly Christian. It is not so much that there are recondite Christian references—though these are plentiful enough—but that the language at such points is at its most thoughtlessly vulgar and sensational:

> O Christ, the spiralling years
> Slither with child and manger to a ball
> Of ice; and what is man? We tear our rags
> To hang the Furies by their itching ears
> And the green needles nail us to the wall.

The assurance with which the elements of this situation are so precisely named (it is a *ball* of ice that is *slithered* to) invites us to visualize what's going on. And yet is the image one can most charitably conjure from these clues anything more than bemusing and pointlessly grotesque and—what really matters—quite inadequate to give force to the rhetorical question it inaugurates? The right to throw out portentous queries like 'what is man?' cannot be lightly claimed and here it is apparent that the poet really doesn't mean any more than what, if anything, that question means; he has been only half-attending to his words' possible reverberations. In his many self-indulgent performances of this sort, Lowell seems as much at the mercy of his words' sound and savagery as the reader is.

Lowell's ear is no more faultless than his tact. His densely alliterative iambic line, its persistent enjambement blocked by compulsively heavy rhyming, too often solidifies into a monotonously high-pitched rhetoric of desperation which can be repellent, particularly where the sense is elusive:

> Under St. Peter's bell the parish sea
> Swells with its smelt into the burlap shack
> Where Joseph plucks his hand-lines like a harp
> And hears the fearful Puer natus est
> Of circumcision, and relieves the wrack
> And howls of Jesus whom he holds. How sharp
> The burden of the Law before the beast:
> Time and the grindstone and the knife of God.
> The child is born in blood, O child of blood.

The words are harsh enough—'wrack', 'howls', 'beast', 'knife' etc.—and there is evidently energy at work amongst them but it is an energy that seems bent on increasing their volume without sharpening their point. Finally the effect is of dullness and even staginess. The poet has put all his money on the individual distinctness and force of his tone of voice; he appears to have trusted that the compulsive pressure of this individual tone will suffice to particularize, to give a personal, hurt edge to a traditionally evocative vocabulary and a crude alliterative tread. Now and then in Lowell, precisely this can happen, but rarely without some supporting advance in concentration, clarity and particularization. In Part 2 of *The Quaker Graveyard in Nantucket*, for example, his subject is the violent confrontation of the Quaker by the retributive energy of the sea, and his properties are drawn from local and literary New England sources and organized so as to give density and pointed resonance to a trained personal experience. In these circumstances, Lowell's vocabulary is held just this side of its characteristically florid crush

and his alliteration is sensitively devised so that in the running battle
it sets up between, broadly, the 's', 'sh', 'w' sounds of the sea and the
'p', 'b' sounds of resistance to the sea, it contrives—for all its hearty
obtrusiveness—a spectacular auditory support to the poem's statement:

> *Whenever winds are moving and their breath*
> *Heaves at the roped-in bulwark of this pier,*
> *The terns and sea-gulls tremble at your death*
> *In these home-waters. Sailor, can you hear*
> *The Pequod's sea-wings, beating landward, fall*
> *Headlong and break on our Atlantic wall*
> *Off 'Sconset, where the yawing S-boats splash*
> *The bell-buoy, with ballooning spinnakers,*
> *As the entangled, screeching mainsheet clears*
> *The blocks; off Madaket, where lubbers lash*
> *The heavy surf and throw their long lead squids*
> *For blue-fish? Sea-gulls blink their heavy lids*
> *Seaward. The winds' wings beat upon the stones,*
> *Cousin, and scream for you and the claws rush*
> *At the sea's throat and wring it in the slush*
> *Of this old Quaker graveyard where the bones*
> *Cry out in the long night for the hurt beast*
> *Bobbing by Ahab's whaleboats in the East.*

Here overflow is inhibited by the presence of concrete facts—place-
names, the cousin whose elegy it is, *Moby Dick*, the nautical terms,
the S-boats, and so on—but one feels that the pressure is towards a
transformation or, more accurately, a wrenching of these facts into
a purely emblematic or rhetorical condition. Randall Jarrell has said
that Lowell sometimes doesn't 'have enough trust in God and tries
to do everything himself'. The world is mistrusted in the same way.

The best of *Lord Weary's Castle* are those poems in which Lowell
has attempted his figure of ultimate retribution and calamity with
the controlling assistance of some local or literary anchor. Readers
of his *Imitations* will not be surprised to find him here drawing

liberally on various literary sources. In *The Quaker Graveyard in Nantucket* Melville and Thoreau are pitted against 'an adaptation of several paragraphs from E. T. Watkins's *Catholic Art and Culture*'. The Thoreau source is one of the innumerable pieces of useful background information that are provided in Hugh B. Staples's *Robert Lowell: The First Twenty Years*. Thoreau writes:

> I saw many many marble feet and matted heads as the clothes were raised, and one livid, swollen, and mangled body of a drowned girl . . . to which some rags still adhered, with a string, half-concealed by the flesh, about its swollen neck; the coiled-up wreck of a human hulk, gashed by the rocks or fishes, so that the bone and muscle were exposed, but quite bloodless—merely red and white—with wide-open and staring eyes, yet lustreless, dead-lights; or like the cabin windows of a stranded vessel, filled with sand. . . .

And Lowell:

> *Light*
> *Flashes from his matted head and marble feet,*
> *He grappled at the net*
> *With the coiled, hurdling muscles of his thighs:*
> *The corpse was bloodless, a botch of reds and whites,*
> *Its open, staring eyes*
> *Were lustreless dead-lights*
> *Or cabin windows on a stranded hulk*
> *Heavy with sand.*

What is admirable here is the sensitivity with which Lowell has selected from Thoreau's lines. By paring down the description of the corpse to the simple 'was bloodless' and by letting the weight of his presentation fall on its 'open, staring eyes', Lowell achieves a shocked, impressionistic vigour which Thoreau—for all his helpful qualifications—fails to carry. Lowell intensifies where Thoreau takes his time. In the other outstanding 'literary' poems, 'The Exiles Return', 'After the Surprising Conversions' and 'Mr. Edwards and the Spider', the same thing occurs. Lowell lends his impassioned speaking voice to intensify a piece of discursive prose which, in its

turn, influences him to curb his rhetoric. Where the source is itself
impassioned, though, Lowell tends to try and go one better—this is
a characteristic of many of his *Imitations*—and this sort of mess can
result (after Villon):

> Now here, now there, the starling and the sea
> Gull splinter the groined eye-balls of my sin,
> Brothers, more beaks of birds than needles in
> The fathoms of the Bayeux Tapestry:
> God wills it, wills it, wills it: it is blood.

But by and large, Lowell's sources have been a help to him, demanding of him both passion and objectivity. They might also have
led him to that increased respect for character and situation which
marks the later poems in *Lord Weary's Castle* and persists through
The Mills of the Kavanaughs (which had its first English publication
as an appendix to Mr. Staples's book) to *Life Studies*. R. P. Blackmur
wrote of Lowell's first published poetry (*Land of Unlikeness*, published in a limited edition of 250 copies in 1944 and partly contained
in *Lord Weary's Castle*): 'in dealing with men his faith compels him
to be fractiously vindictive, and in dealing with faith his experience
of men compels him to be nearly blasphemous', and it is true that in
the majority of the poems in *Lord Weary's Castle*, Boston exists as a
moral emblem; Lowell uses its signposts for polemical purposes but
the people are nowhere to be found. With the Jonathan Edwards
poems, though, and 'Between the Porch and the Altar', a new
interest in narrative emerges. The opening lines of 'Katherine's
Dream', for instance, are like nothing else in *Lord Weary's Castle*:

> It must have been a Friday. I could hear
> The top-floor typist's thunder and the beer
> That you had brought in cases hurt my head;
> I'd sent the pillows flying from my bed,
> I hugged my knees together and I gasped.

But even in these, the calmest of Lowell's early lines, one can detect
that debilitating antagonism between the rhetorical and the narrative

motive which is to become centrally ruinous in the dramatic monologues of *The Mills of the Kavanaughs* volume. 'You feel that the
people are made up', Lowell has said of Browning (*Paris Review*
interview, Spring 1961), 'you feel there's a glaze between what he
writes and what really happened', that he lacks 'some kind of sympathy and observation of people'. This is true of Lowell's own
dramatic monologues. His advance in subject matter is not accom-
panied by a substantial variation of manner or broadening of emotional range. Although the Catholic symbolism is less obtrusive and
some attempt is being made to take people seriously, the characters
are still the horribly punished, the suicidal. They are still fallen and
theological. Great poetry can get written about madness but there is
no such thing as great madness. Composure must at least be looked,
or yearned for and it must be more integral than the mere formality
which the aping of traditional verse forms can effect. With Lowell
there is a sense in which even this formality is present only to be
disgraced. The learned hysteria of *The Mills of the Kavanaughs* is the
culmination of Lowell's apocalyptic vein (only 'Falling Asleep over
the Aeneid' achieves anything like the powered restraint of the best
of *Lord Weary's Castle*) and with it he seems to realize that his full-
blooded gestural rhetoric is too uniformly emphatic an instrument
for handling the problems of narrative and too monotonously
single-pitched for objective or dramatic representations of human
behaviour and the sorts of secular situation in which he is becoming
interested. It was perhaps considerations of this sort, together with
what seems to have been Lowell's de-conversion from Roman
Catholicism (recorded in 'Beyond the Alps?') which brought about
the radical change of style that characterizes most of the verse in *Life
Studies*. Searching for a 'break-through back into life', Lowell
abandons his tight metric, indeed abandons any sort of formality of
line, and writes a verse that is loose, subdued and prosaic, full of fine
perceptions and richly disconsolate in tone, but, as Colin Falck has
admirably pointed out already in *The Review*, quite disorganized.

The autobiographical poems in *Life Studies* act as elaborations of
certain characters and incidents in Lowell's prose autobiography, a

fragment of which was printed alongside in the American edition.
Here is some prose:

> Almost immediately he bought a larger and more stylish house;
> he sold his ascetic stove-black Hudson and bought a plump brown
> Buick; later the Buick was exchanged for a high-toned, as-good-
> as-new Packard with a custom-designed royal blue and mahogany
> body. Without drama, his earnings more or less decreased from
> year to year.

And here, a verse account of the same events:

> *whenever he left a job,*
> *he bought a smarter car.*
> *Father's last employer*
> *was Scudder, Stevens and Clark, Investment Advisers,*
> *himself his only client.*
> *While Mother dragged to bed alone,*
> *read Menninger,*
> *and grew more and more suspicious,*
> *he grew defiant.*
> *Night after night,*
> *à la clarté déserte de sa lampe,*
> *he slid his ivory Annapolis slide rule*
> *across a pad of graphs—*
> *piker speculations! In three years*
> *he squandered sixty thousand dollars.*

There is no reason why the first of these passages should be set out
as prose and the second syntactically line-broken into verse: indeed,
the first passage acts upon the reader more 'poetically'—that is, the
colours and the car-names are allowed to do the work and there is
none of the chattiness that distends the second. The closing com-
ments on Father's earnings could be interchanged without anything
being lost either way.

On the whole, the explicitly autobiographical poems in *Life
Studies* add little except further information to the prose. It might
ultimately be possible to see them as precisely the sort of low-pres-

sure exploration of his Boston past that Lowell was in need of to lend
some specific resonance to his discontent. Certainly, a recent poem
like 'For the Union Dead' is an encouraging sign in this direction: it
shows Lowell returning to the Boston legend with an objective
malice, a detail and variety of local reference and a sharpened sense
of public responsibility. Henry James's remarks about Hawthorne
are truer of the later than of the early Lowell:

> It is only in a country where newness and change and brevity of
> tenure are the common substance of life, that the fact of one's
> ancestors having lived for a hundred and seventy years in a single
> spot would become an element of one's morality. It is only an
> imaginative American that would feel urged to keep reverting to
> this circumstance, to keep analysing and cunningly considering it.

Lowell's attitude to Boston has not grown up to analysis and cunning without a considerable loss in intensity: he is now faced with
the problem of recapturing something of his early vigour. The
melodramatic gestures of despair that infiltrate some of his most
recent poems ('I am tired. Everyone's tired of my turmoil') and run
through *Imitations* are an attempt towards this end, perhaps. *Imitations* itself does not represent a significant advance: it 'was written
from time to time when I was unable to do anything of my own'
and for all the freedom of these renderings ('from Homer to Pasternak'), their brilliant original flashes, they are, substantially, not anything of his own. One must still look to *Life Studies* for a clue to
Lowell's future, to 'Waking in the Blue', 'Man and Wife', 'Memories
of West Street and Lepke' and particularly to the sort of achievement
that is represented by these lines from 'Home After Three Months
Away'. Here, what is seen is transformed but not violated by what
is understood, there is an intimate collaboration of exploratory and
rhetorical energies, and the measurement is by a voice that is memorably personal and contemporary.

> *Recuperating, I neither spin nor toil.*
> *Three stories down below,*
> *a choreman tends our coffin's length of soil,*

and seven horizontal tulips blow.
Just twelve months ago,
those flowers were pedigreed
imported Dutchmen, now no one need
distinguish them from weed.
Bushed by the late spring snow,
they cannot meet
another year's snowballing enervation.
I keep no rank or station.
Cured, I am frizzled stale and small.

1963

2. For the Union Dead

With *Life Studies*, for all its fine moments, it was difficult to see how Robert Lowell would break out of what seemed to be a technical as well as an emotional deadlock; he was right, certainly, to have escaped the agonized, over-packed iambic line, the constraints which his energy could only quarrel with, and it was good to see him discovering Boston in personal not theological terms—there was, throughout the book, a general access of humane warmth and delicate perception. But there also seemed to be a leisured, digressive tendency in his new manner; the detail flooded in and he often seemed too helpless and devout with it, too reluctant to intervene and fashion into autonomous poetic shape material that was so nakedly authentic, so irretrievably lost should he—its sole guardian —neglect or tamper with it.

As Williams's *Paterson* testifies, this kind of individual labour of conservation is endless and can be just as wasteful as the forces it proposes to defy. What one missed in the family-history poems in *Life Studies*—in spite of the almost emblematic significance that the Lowell family has in the American conscience—was some encouragement that the past might yield to poetry not just its fugitive detail but something of its essential imagery. In *For the Union Dead* the past weighs just as heavily on Lowell as it did in *Life Studies* but here one is involved in rather more than the poet's private, touching excavations; what is revealed is Lowell's despairing recognition that he has failed to make sense out of the fragments of his history which he both hoards and flees.

The extremes of Lowell's poetry are still those of paradise and purgatory, though, and for both he has the language; 'We know how the world will end/but where is paradise', he writes, and it is against the dislocated anguish of poems like 'Night Sweat', 'The Drinker' and 'Myopia: A Night' that he opposes those moments of passionate, nostalgic recall that blaze up in 'Old Flame', 'Water', 'The Lesson'. 'Remember we sat on a slab of rock?', 'Remember our list of birds?', 'Remember Summer?'; this becomes as insistent a note as the 'Back and forth, back and forth' of his sinister clocks. But, it must always be admitted, 'A father's no shield/for his child', 'Our end is nearer', and it is still Jonathan Edwards's 'wild spiders crying together' who are doomed to nuclear extinction, who must crack up, or take to drink, or cling in desperation to the imagery that can merely measure their plight. Of Hawthorne, Lowell writes:

> Leave him alone for a moment or two,
> and you'll see him with his head
> bent down, brooding, brooding
> eyes fixed on some chip,
> some stone, some common plant,
> the commonest thing,
> as if it were a clue.
> The disturbed eyes rise,
> furtive, foiled, dissatisfied
> from meditation on the true
> and insignificant.

It often seems that this is how Lowell is obliged to regard his own meditations. It is the intensity with which he concentrates upon what he calls 'the stabbing detail', demanding from it at least 'the universal that belonged to this detail and nowhere else', that gives his poetry its rich, visual accuracy; and the current of pain and nervous horror in which these images seem incessantly to stand entranced—this seems often to arise from his acknowledgement that he will perhaps fail to find in what he sees anything more than a meaningless, obsessive vigour.

As with Hawthorne, there are two senses in which Lowell's eye is 'disturbed'; his past will not allow him the innocent traffic with nature such as a poet like Williams seems to him to have enjoyed, and yet he feels that he has sucked his conscience dry. His inheritance has dwindled to the involuntary habit of expecting from the world what he knows it cannot afford, of searching for heaven when he knows full well that he is confined to hell. It is in this sense, perhaps —although, as always with Lowell, it is also the literal truth—that he has 'a glazed eye', 'a distracted eye'; in poem after poem, this crops up—'some mote, some eye-flaw wobbles in the heat', 'all's ramshackle, streaky, wierd/for the near-sighted', 'the old cut cornea throbbed' and so on. As a child, he read his Bible, 'till the page turned black' and he was brought up to note 'the darker passages'; 'Young, my eyes began to fail'.

In an obituary article on William Carlos Williams (*The Hudson Review*, Winter, 1961), Lowell gave an indication of the kind of imaginative process that now seems most important to him. It is, I think, worth quoting:

> When I think of writing about Dr. Williams, I feel a chaos of thoughts and images, images cracking open to admit a thought, thoughts dragging their roots for the soil of an image. When I woke up this morning, something unusual for summer was going on!—pinpricks of rain were falling in a reliable, comforting simmer. Our town was blanketed in the rain of rot and the rain of renewal. New life was muscling in, everything growing moved on its one-way trip to the ground. I could feel this, yet believe our universal misfortune was bearable and even welcome. An image held my mind during these moments and kept returning —an old-fashioned New England cottage, freshly painted white. I saw a triangular shade on the house, trees, a hedge, or their shadows, a blotch of decay. The house might have been the

house I was living in but it wasn't; it came from the time when I
was a child, still unable to read and living in the small town of
Barnstaple on Cape Cod. Inside the house was a birdbook with an
old stiff and steely engraving of a sharp-skinned hawk. The
hawk's legs had a reddish brown buffalo fuzz on them; behind
was the blue sky bare and abstracted from the world. In the
present, pinpricks of rain were falling on everything I could see,
and even on the white house in my mind, but the hawk's picture,
being indoors I suppose, was more or less spared. Since I saw the
picture of the hawk, the pinpricks of rain have gone on, half the
people I once knew are dead, half the people I now know were
unborn, and I have learned to read.

In the poem 'Eye and Tooth' which Lowell derives from this passage (and which I wish I had the space to quote fully since it shows
how Lowell's handling of the autobiographical prose source has
matured and sharpened since the often very limp selections in *Life
Studies*), the hawk's message is the Biblical 'an eye for an eye, a tooth
for a tooth' and it was in the hawk's service, possibly, that the child
ruined his eyes and left his tooth ('noosed in a knot to the door-
knob') in the New England house which now 'nothing can dislodge'
and which is yet touched by the general process of 'rot and renewal'.
It is not Lowell's method to offer any precise discursive weight to
images like that of the hawk, nor to explicate the grounds on which
he feels himself to be suffering some kind of penance at its hands—
for a lesson too thoroughly learned, or too easily betrayed, for a too-
fierce dedication to God, to Art, to ends 'abstracted from the world'?
The cottage, the birdbook, the triangular blotch of decay are not
mere allegorical tokens but are felt to be profoundly ingrained elements of the poet's morality, and untranslatable; they press upon
him as in some way an important aspect and perhaps the source of
his present desolation but they will not surrender to the explicating
intelligence. They are, simply, the 'soil of an image' in which
Lowell finds his thoughts 'dragging their roots'.
    And this is a fair way of describing how most of the poems in
this book seem to work; by a shading, echoing, reverberating
process the images seek each other out and are interpenetrated

in a structure tight enough to encompass their full range of connotation. Very little is allowed to spill over, to preen itself or to wander off on its own, and however desperate the tone, one is usually aware of Lowell's craftsmanlike discrimination at the back of it.

In his title poem, for instance, there is the minimum of abstraction or actual comment; the poem feels its way concretely, image by image, so that what seems at first a local outrage intensifies to reveal itself as a profound disturbance in the whole of nature, an 'earth-quake', 'a Sahara of snow', a nuclear explosion, a dinosaur eating its way into the heart of America, and so on. The poem's actual event is the digging of a subterranean garage in Boston; to withstand this assault the old Statehouse is braced with girders, the Civil War monument is 'propped by a plank splint'. But the city, the best of its values, are being undermined, it is 'tingling' and 'shaking' and will not survive the shock, any more than the 'Mosler Safe', the 'Rock of Ages' will withstand a nuclear explosion; the fish that Lowell used to watch swimming behind glass in the old South Boston Aquarium, now derelict and boarded up—its 'bronze weathervane cod has lost half its scales'—have given way to the 'giant finned cars' that 'nose forward like fish'. The glass of the Aquarium has yielded to the glass of the television screen on which 'the drained faces of Negro schoolchildren rise like balloons'; little wonder that the monument to Colonel Shaw's Negro infantry now 'sticks like a fishbone/in the city's throat'. These relations are handled very subtly and it would take an essay on its own to show the full extent of Lowell's skill in this poem; what really impresses, though, is that even with this much detectable craft the thing still seems very natural, a deeply personal, spoken elegy for those images, both private and public, that have meant most to the poet and that are now steeling themselves for extinction:

> On a thousand small town New England greens,
> of old white churches hold their air
> of sparse, sincere rebellion; frayed flags

> quilt the graveyard of the Grand
> Army of the Republic.
>
> The stone statues of the abstract
> Union Soldier
> grow slimmer and younger each year—
> wasp-waisted, they doze over muskets
> and muse through their sideburns . . .

If there is anyone who still doubts that Robert Lowell is the most important poet now writing in English, then a book that can maintain this quality in nearly every poem ought surely to set him right.

1965

3. *Notebook*

In a 'Note to the New Edition' of *Notebook*, Robert Lowell tells us that in the six months or so between the publication of the book's American edition and the preparation of the text for English readers, he made alterations to 'about a hundred of the old poems' and added more than ninety new ones. He treated, he says, his published work (the American edition) as a manuscript. On the page facing this explanatory note, Lowell gives a list of the uglier historical landmarks of the last three years—'The Six Days War, first week in June, 1967', 'Martin Luther King's Murder, April 4, 1968', 'Robert Kennedy's Murder, June 5, 1968', 'The Russian Occupation of Czechoslovakia, August 21, 1968', and so on—and justifies the inclusion of this *aide-mémoire* as follows: 'Dates fade faster than we do. Many in the last two years are already gone; in a year or two the rest will slip.'

Together, these concluding notes constitute a kind of apologia for the method of the total work we have just read. They speak of haste, the haste with which awful events arrive and pass away, the haste with which the poet-diarist must register them on his pulses before it is too late, the ensuing haste of both composition and revision. And in that rush, it is implied, the artist can attend but patchily to art's rush-refusing obligations. Lowell attends a good deal less patchily than any other poet would have in the circumstances, and it is this that makes the book depressing: *Notebook* is just rich enough to keep reminding us of what is being wasted. Lowell has written carelessly in the past, he has always been prone to over-exploit his best gifts and to allow his linguistic fertility to outpace his impulse. But nowhere in his earlier work—except maybe in *The Mills of the Kavanaughs*—has he surrendered so forlornly to self-parody, the strenuous but machine-like animation of dead mannerisms, as he does throughout this volume.

In the age of the short poem, the poet seeking to be called ambitious will be tempted to package his brevities in the form of a sequence. He will then insist that this sequence is not what it seems to be—a random bundling of independent works—but is in fact a 'single poem'. John Berryman's *Dream Songs* offers a key instance of this kind of marketing, and Lowell has confessed to having got the idea for *Notebook* from that 'poem'. In the same way, just as Berryman tailors his individual songs to a strict, if strictly arbitrary, pattern, so Lowell here elects to allot each of his poems-within-the-poem a ration of fourteen lines (rhyme and metre optional). And just as Berryman challenged us, teasingly, to contemplate the possibility of structure in what he had done, Lowell too advances his collection as 'one poem, intuitive in pattern'. That 'intuitive' is, of course, a way of warning us that, although we ought to look for patterns, we ought not to be surprised if we don't find them.

Thus structure, both overall and as it is applied to individual poems, is employed as a receptacle, a spacious bin that can take and tidy anything the poet chooses to dump in it. And although we may never grasp the total pattern, individual poems—because they are offered as part of a pattern—can be as flat, ragged and inconsequential as they happen to turn out. Arbitrarily curtailed after fourteen lines, they can simply bump to a halt—after all, they do not *finish* there. The effect of the accumulative strategy is to permit the poet to abdicate from actually completing anything, and thus from the need to ever ask himself if what he has written is in fact a poem. The internal organization, the rhythmic and imagistic shaping, the dramatic pace and timing of the single poem: these become optional objectives also.

Here and there, in *Notebook*, one can disembed poems in which Lowell has seen such objectives as essential, and some of these—see poems 3 and 4 from the 'Through the Night' section—are as beautiful, as beautifully *made*, as anything Lowell has written. But how rarely, from a close-spaced book of over 250 pages, can this be said. The vast majority of the poems are, simply, shoddy; shoddy in one or another of the many ways that Lowell can now be so; in ways, that is to say, which do not necessarily eschew intelligence or cultivation or, even, the eruption intermittently of an image or a cadence or a four-line burst that only a poet of his genius could have been subject to. The real shoddiness of *Notebook* is that time and again it debases into facility the poet's most potent qualities. The tightly conversational voice is frittered into chatter, the heartfelt, in extremis, plaint sounds thin, forced and vain, the appetite for history, for heroes and detritus, becomes gluttonous and indiscriminate.

But worst of all, Lowell's powers of language have degenerated into a ready-for-anything rhetorical machine; you name it, I'll write it up with urgent vigour. Consider the three-adjective device, once surprising and supple, but now trundled out mechanically: 'over-white, over-observed, ignored', 'angular, night-bluish, blear-eyed, spinsterish', 'elastic, curved and cool', 'each day more brutal, oracular and rooted', 'poised warm and cool'. One could list dozens; and note with each, despondently, that not one of them is *bad*. Consider too the empty, flogged melodrama: 'Revolution/dragging her terrible pre-menstrual cramps/marches with unbra'd breasts to storm the city', 'Earth, the great beast, clanks its chain of vertebrae'; the slickly colourful, but essentially unseen, descriptive thrusts: 'Your sinewy lips wide-eyed as the honey-comb/your tongue as smooth as truth'; the philosophical banalities: 'the poverty all men must face at the hour of death', 'laws imprison as much as they protect'; the sleek agonizing: 'the soul groans and laughs at its lack of stature'.

The temptation to shrug off such things and to point instead to (what, admittedly, needs mentioning) the work's size, range, assimilative energy and so on (it moves back and forth through the poet's autobiography, hymning dead friends, lost loves, and heroes ancient and modern, against a backcloth of contemporary political misfortune and the despair of an individual haunted by his own griefs and nostalgias) would be a mistake, for it seems to have been in pursuit, in easy expectation of, such applause that this fine poet has allowed himself to let things slip—as life slips, and with it life's applause.

1970

John Berryman

Even the most confirmed admirers of John Berryman's *77 Dream Songs* have been obliged to concede beginners' lists of the bits from this new sequence that make some sense, and to confess that much of it is impenetrable, either artfully or crazily; there has been surprisingly little attempt, though, to seriously challenge Berryman's plea that the work has some kind of structural direction. The songs are presented as 'one version of a poem in progress'. Do we believe this, or are we being led by the nose?

Determining the relationship that exists between the diverse tendencies of his work has always been the problem with Berryman, and his earlier verse hardly encourages trust in his certainty of purpose. In his poetry of the thirties and of the war years, work of despondent, haphazard social comment or of impassioned recoil from the 'evil waste of history outstretched', there is not only the disabling debt to Auden forever leaving its mark but, more seriously in terms of his future development, there is a strange tendency to infiltrate the bald and rather trite solemnities which his poems keep running into, and which they really seem meant for, with gratuitous comedies of tone and syntax. It is often almost as if the poems were being composed with two hands, the one seeking to correct the other's bad habits. This is more than a surface muddle; it seems that basic to it in many cases there runs an important confusion of motive.

For example, a poem like 'The Disciple', a monologue on Christ's teaching, doesn't seem to know, or finally to care, how seriously it wishes to be taken. It borrows heavily, but not consistently, from the relaxed, illuminated retrospection of Eliot's 'Journey of the Magi', and its climax is direct praise:

Great nonsense has been spoken of that time,

> *But I can tell you I saw then*
> *A terrible darkness on the face of men,*
> *His last astonishment; and now that I'm*
> *Old I behold it as a young man yet.*
> *None of us know now what it means,*
> *But to this day our loves and disciplines*
> *Worry themselves there. We do not forget.*

In spite of the echoes, the stock turns of phrase and the wartime
memorial note of the last line, the effort here seems to be for direct
simplicity and warmth—though 'worry themselves' might be more
loaded than it seems—a development of what has been said earlier
in the poem of 'the warm sad cadence' of Christ's voice, his compassion for 'the indigent and crippled of this town'. Now if this were
all the poem had to offer, it could be taken as a dull, rather fumbling
hymn; but alongside all the routine piety there is evidence of a quite
different feeling about the subject. The verse before the one I have
just quoted describes the betrayal and the crucifixion in a bright,
punning style, offhand and full of fun:

> *I was among them, but one whom*
> *He harboured kissed him for the coppers' doom.*
> *Repenting later most most bitterly,*
> *They ran him down and drove him up the hill.*
> *He who had lifted but hearts stood*
> *With thieves, performing still what tricks he could*
> *For men to come, rapt in compassion still.*

The puns cluster and jostle; 'harboured'—protecting from the law,
and providing, literally, a haven: the copper-policemen who judged
or doomed Christ are themselves judged and doomed, the copper-
coins that were paid for his betrayal were the instrument of this
doom, and usually are; 'ran him down'—they spoke disparagingly
of him, they hunted and caught him; 'drove him up the hill'—they
herded him there, the shepherd, or the modern coppers took him
there in their modern cars, but the lines also hint of the nails driven

into Christ's hands and feet; 'lifted'—as in shoplift or uplift; 'for
men to come'—in historical terms, so that the men would come and
watch his latest trick, but universally, for the benefit of future
humanity; 'rapt in compassion still'—refers to men of the time, men
now and Christ himself. And so on. One could play for hours, but
without getting any closer to grasping the central point of all this
double-talk.

It is a joke, perhaps, but on whom? On Christ, on the doomed
coppers, on 'men to come', or on the joker himself? Is Berryman
here mimicking a shallowness that he disapproves of, ironically
undermining the rhetoric that is to follow, or is he trying to work
out a real hesitation of intent which the final stanza can be held to
resolve. There is surely no way of telling. Throughout the poem
Christ has been shown as both conjurer and saint—the disciple has
felt both 'terror of his choice' and a rather lordly mystification at the
way this 'ventriloquist and strolling mage' took the hearts of
'respectable citizens' and

> *swashed them in an upland brook*
> *Calling them his, all men's, anonymous.*

One can see ways in which just this sort of ambivalence could have
made a subtle, interwoven poem; an aggressive cheapening of the
longed-for event must have seemed one way of coping with it and
perhaps is now the only way—maybe this is more or less what
Berryman means to say. But done like this—the piety pulling the
chair from beneath the wisecracks, and vice versa—one is bound to
wonder where the poem's centre really is, and to ask if Berryman
isn't really just floundering.

I have concentrated on this single poem because it puts in a usefully crude way what is a typical puzzle in Berryman. At times he is
the statue, the dark watcher, the prophet, extending a dignified
compassion to the 'homosexuals, the crippled, the alone'. Like
Auden he plays a Christ who has spotted the 'motives in the corri-
dor', the 'violence in rooms', and yet can tell us of 'the coming
good', 'the thaw'. Cold weather provides him with a constant image

H

of the time's *paraplegia dolorosa*: 'snow howls', 'icy speculae float', and 'our sorrow among steel and glass' is necessarily touched by the shadow of 'the massive sorrow of the mental hospital'. The poet's generation inherits the 'violent world our fathers bought' and must now pay for it 'with fantasy at dawn'. Berryman's symptomatizing to this end is often inert and obvious and is never really sharpened by the keen, inspecting eye it often affects. The Freudianism that directs it is usually pedestrian and obtrusive, as in 'Desires of Men and Women', where 'half-lit and lascivious apartments' are shown to be in fact the secret goal of those who live with 'old silver, lace and privacy' and who practise the aristocratic graces, and rather later in 'Song of the Bridegroom' (one of the *Nervous Songs* that prefigure his *Dream Songs*), the bridegroom is presented as longing to 'be laid away, felted in depths of caves' and marriage is very cornily described as 'like a journey home/Frightening after so distant years'.

The loftily comprehending and piteous role never seems really to suit Berryman. Not only does he fail to discover an idiom of his own in which he can handle such general wisdom but the preaching impulse usually leads him into an awkward, near-prose delivery that gets clotted at the ends of lines or bogged down in syntactical muddles. It is not only the borrowed voice that makes these lines from 'The Statue' troublesome; it is also a kind of fretting for the spaciousness of prose:

> *Where I sit, near the entrance to the Park,*
> *The charming dangerous entrance to their need,*
> *Dozens, a hundred men have lain till morning*
> *And the preservative darkness waning,*
> *Waking to want, to the day before, desire*
> *For the ultimate good.*

The restraint seems cruelly self-imposed, and in Berryman's idealization of art's 'sleepless justifying ruined stare' one comes close to understanding why. The detachment can quicken into isolation, the solicitude into despair, and the sharp social comment into disgusted condemnation. It is not just the predicament of those millions 'whose

happiness runs out like water', whose walk in the park is coming to
an end, that is made to seem pitiable in this poem, but also the predicament of the artist whom they ignore, who cannot truthfully
attend them as he would wish—with fine assurances of that 'ultimate good'. Where the poem goes wrong is that in taking on such
a labour of diagnosis and compassion, by in fact assuming the responsibility which it acknowledges cannot be fulfilled, it seems to
disguise the true direction of its interests. One is left, as so often,
wondering where Berryman wants his sympathies to seem to lie.

In 'Animal Trainer' he explicitly faces this kind of conflict, and
concludes as one might expect. The trainer wants to abandon his
animals and embark on some private spiritual journey to 'a suburb
of the spirit' where he could seize the 'steady and exalted light of the
sun'. His heart, though, reminds him of what he owes to the animals:
'your love and your immense responsibility'. There may be a
'bloodless pride' in living 'like an artist in the sun', and it may seem
futile to feel responsible for those who

> *run*
> *into forbidden corners, they fight, they steal*

but animal trainers have to acknowledge, in the end, that animals
must be 'your destruction and your will'. The argument could
hardly be put more explicitly, nor could the resolution be much
more tight-lipped, but it is significant that Berryman should have
written the poem at all. The very analogy, between animal training
and the responsibilities of the artist, seems to carry its own con-
temptuous contradiction of the poem's avowed concern; the barren,
dispirited language signals the dead end of Berryman's attempt for a
warm, sad, responsible poetry of direct social comment.

The way out had to be drastic, and the long poem, *Homage to
Mistress Bradstreet*, represents the final abandonment of all that is
ponderous and straightforward in early Berryman, and the culmination of that freelancing, idiosyncratic vein which had hitherto
seemed either throttled or pointlessly self-indulgent. In it Berryman breaks free both from his old style and from the commitments

which had encouraged that style. He systematically evolves a poetic language which is remote from ordinary speech, having its roots perhaps, via Hopkins, in the diction of Edward Taylor, the most considerable of America's seventeenth-century Colonial school. Taylor is ecstatic, vigorously self-mortifying, intricately clever, and he rejoices in the tortuous ways of syntax as they seem to mirror the tortuous ways of the black, aspiring soul; though he might try to 'weave with an angelick skill/A Damask web of Velvet Verse', it wouldn't work:

> *all my web would run*
> *To rags and jags; so snick-snarled to the thrum*

This is not a bad way of describing Berryman's own style as he pays homage to Taylor's contemporary, Anne Bradstreet. The archaistic pose is clear enough, and the work is riddled with obscurities that seem to arise directly from compressions and transitions that could happily have been made more supple; the ampersands, the accents, the antiquated past-participles, the alliteration—all seem carried well beyond the point where they might be said to have had some real usefulness, and often have the appearance of mere self-indulgent fun. The notes, too, are mocking riddles, largely, and there is enough self-parading naughtiness throughout the whole enterprise to seriously disturb.

Berryman does not explicitly match his world with Anne Bradstreet's, or send her messages; he attempts, briefly, to inhabit and vitalize her imagination, to discover, through her, what it felt like to be present at the first moment of poetry in the first hostile America. For the English reader, this America might seem remote and narrow, but for the American, as Lowell also testifies, it is the source from which many of his trials proceed. Where Lowell plunges modern Boston into a Calvinist hell, Berryman recreates the origins of the American effort to make poetry out of a hostile, anti-poetic social context. If Bradstreet failed where Taylor succeeded, then it was that her true energies and agonies were never allowed to find their way into poetry in the way that Taylor's managed to. Taylor never published, but she did, conscious presumably of the standards of an intellectual milieu dominated by the rigours of Wigglesworth's *Day of Doom*:

> *all this bald*
> *abstract didactic rime I read appalled*

Berryman writes to her. She is 'mistress neither of fiery nor velvet verse' but appears always on her knees, 'hopeful and shamefast, chaste, laborious, odd'. Her most famous poem is 'To My Dear and Loving Husband'—it is devout and sweetly subservient, and yet Berryman doubts

> *if Simon than this blast, that sea*
> *spares from his rigour for your poetry more.*

He approaches her not only as a fellow poet, as one who understands and shares what she must really have felt,

> *we are on each other's hands*
> *who care. Both of our worlds unhanded us*

but also as the terrifying, longed-for lover. It is Anne's thirst for a consuming experience of love, a full creativity of spirit, and her appalling guilt that she should want this, that is Berryman's central assumption about her. Her desire is shown to be stifled and menaced by the rigid codes of the society in which she has found herself; the experience of childbirth—she had eight children—is the only release into the violent, triumphant, 'natural' element that Berryman wishes for her, and is certainly a way of cleansing for a while from her life all that is crabbed and morosely zealous. Anne, at fourteen, had found her heart to be 'carnal and sitting loose from God' and when the Lord returned to claim her, 'the pox blasted' and left her skin 'cratered . . . like the crabs and shells of my Palissy ewer'. She married 'so-much-older Simon' when she was sixteen and travelled with him to the New World two years later.

From finding her 'Pockmarkt and westward staring on a haggard deck', Berryman traces her early years in America, her first tough

winter, the birth of her first child, her homesickness, her general
restiveness and her moments of tense commitment to her tasks as
wife, mother and pilgrim; her voice then meets with his in an
almost hysterical dialogue of temptation and guilt that has
moments of extraordinary power. Here, for instance, where Anne's
capitulation almost seems to bleed into a lust for its proper, its
deserved punishment:

> *I see the cruel spread Wings black with saints!*
> *Silky my breasts not his, mine, mine to withold*
> *or tender, tender.*
> *I am sifting, nervous and bold.*
> *The light is changing. Surrender this loveliness*
> *you cannot make me do. But I will. Yes.*
> *What horror, down stormy air,*
> *warps towards me? My threatening promise faints*
> *torture me, Father, lest not I be thine!*
> *Tribunal terrible and pure, my God*
> *mercy for him and me.*

It is at moments like these that Berryman's style seems absolutely
appropriate to its subject. The word-order, though odd and engi-
neered, is yet touchingly right. Halting, stunned, child-like—something important would be lost, one feels, by having it done differently. As in 'Brood I do on myself naked', 'Harmless I to you/am
not, not I', one can see that the near-asphyxiated, blushing, surge of
energy is what Berryman is after, and achieves.

Anne's situation, of course, serves as a means for Berryman to
explore his own American-ness, as well as to focus his view of himself as an artist plagued by the demands of a world that has no real
place for him, driven by that old desire to 'stand naked in the sun'
in some absolute visionary stance, yet menaced still by that puri-
tanical self-disgust that broke through in his early poems in lines
like 'all this biting and breeding', 'clap of remorse and tang and
fang', and so on. To set alongside *Bradstreet* a poem like 'Canto
Amor' is illuminating. In this, a straight-forward love poem, the

'Unknown Majesty' is praised for a beloved who is 'pale as a star', 'like chords, a sacrifice', who 'seemed to fill the lilac shadow with light' and whose hair is 'fire gold/not earthly hair'; she is herself the Unknown Majesty, and that in turn becomes Art itself. To attempt to work out Berryman's 'beliefs' with the help of either poem would be a fairly thankless task.

In Berryman's next volume, 77 Dream Songs, his alienation is even more extreme, and his style, maintaining as it does most of the peculiarities that one finds in Homage to Mistress Bradstreet but lacking the exact point it had there, seems even more wilfully corrupt. The Dream Songs are spoken by one Henry, whose voice shades into that of Mr. Bones and of the poet himself. Between them they engage in a long, meandering collocation of reverie, back-chat, flat lament, obituary, prayer; 'coon-talk' breaks into ornate rhetoric, literary allusiveness yields to stuttering baby-language. Much of the time the language seems either suicidally self-engrossed or murderously affected. Henry spills his hints over a dozen important areas, politics, literature, psycho-analysis, history, racial prejudice, etc., but does so with a mad disregard for poetry. There is no sustained, mastering recreation of experience but more a frenzied gesticulation at the God who has left things as messy and absurd as Berryman's sequence makes them seem. Poetry could hardly make sense out of what God has given up for lost is what this kind of demented, self-tormenting demolition of the language seems to take for granted:

> Supreme my holdings, greater yet my need,
> thoughtless I go out. Dawn. Have my cigs
> my flaskie O,
> O crystal cock—my kneel has gone to seed—
> and anybody's blessing? (Blast the MIGs
> for making fumble so
> my tardy readying.)

There seems now a silly relish in the disordering of syntax; in the last three lines here it does nothing, except sustain a habit that has become mechanical. One could cite scores of instances of the same kind of thing.

Henry is presented at the outset of the sequence as the victim of some unnamed calamity that has upset his world:

> All the world like a woollen lover
> once did seem on Henry's side

Now, the poet promises, he is to be 'pried open for all the world to see'. Any attempt to push much further than this for a general scheme behind the songs seems doomed to failure. Henry does not emerge as a character, nor as a potent mask, but as the sum of the various frightening or comic gestures that are attributed to him. His features accumulate, as do his vague troubles, his delusions, his moments of panic and boredom, but they do not finally cohere into any memorable dramatic shape.

Henry, we gather, is a scholar, a writer of 'mad books', a movie-fan, and he is tired of the 'squeamish comfy ruin-prone national mind'. He is 'at odds wif de world and its god' and 'is ready to move on'. At the same time, though, he can habitually ask:

> Vouchsafe me, Sleepless One,
> a personal experience of the body of Mrs Boogry
> before I pass from lust

or

> Hurl, God who found
> us in this, down
> something . . . we hear the more
> sin has increased, the more
> grace has been caused to abound

It is between these two familiar poles of his 'ruin-prone mind' that Henry's aspirations and defeats are bewilderingly experienced.

His most effective role is that of the cartoon figure of the little man, hungry and adrift in the urban jungle; he clowns and bleakly cross-talks with Mr. Bones, dreams that he is Humphrey Bogart,

yearns for girls in restaurants. In these songs he seems to have the
makings of a memorable pathetic hero, and Berryman handles him
with more assurance and control than one can recognize in the less
light-weight pieces:

> *Filling her compact and delicious body*
> *with chicken paprika, she glanced at me*
> *twice.*
> *fainting with interest, I hungered back*
> *and only the fact of her husband and four other people*
> *kept me from springing on her*
> *or falling at her little feet and crying*
> *'You are the hottest one for years of night*
> *Henry's dazed eyes*
> *have enjoyed, Brilliance' I advanced upon*
> *(despairing) my spumoni.*

There are many such engaging flashes of this kind throughout, and
the *Songs* are just about worth ploughing through to find them.
Indeed, it is a pity that Berryman did not elect to make more of this
mode—there is a fluent intensification from this sort of wry self-
appraisal to the more desolate confession of, for instance, Song 29.
Unfortunately, Henry is rarely this available; most often he is
boringly mad, or madly clever, or stumbling over his absurd
prayers—and the language he employs has less to do with poetry
than it has to do with 'Mr. Heartbreak, the New Man/Come to
farm the crazyland'.

1965

The Sixties Press

The American Sixties Press enterprise is worth watching; it represents a deliberate reaction against academic knottiness, the Objectivist clarities and the vandalism of the Beat Generation. Its leading poets, Robert Bly and James Wright, have turned to European (Spanish and German), South American and Chinese sources for models of what Bly looks forward to as the 'period of surrealism' which American poetry has yet to fully experience. 'The kind of poetry that has been developed in Europe and South America is a poetry in which the image comes forward and much more is said by suggestion. The subconscious and the unconscious are brought forward in the poetry.' Bly said this in a radio interview and in his introduction to a recently published collection of Sixties Press poetry, *The Lion's Tail and Eyes* ('We have to understand that the rest of the lion is there'), he makes it clear that by 'the image' he doesn't mean what the Imagists or Pound meant by it: 'The poetry of pictures is very good for describing the outer world . . . the fundamental world of poetry is, however, the inward world.' Of course, Pound never wanted anything so crude as a 'poetry of pictures' and his theories readily accommodated what Bly calls 'the inward world', but one gets the point—it is the hardness, the definiteness of visual experience that is being called in question.

For Robert Bly, who runs the press and edits a lively quarterly—*The Sixties* (from Odin House, Madison, Minnesota, U.S.A.)—poetry should create fresh experience out of the materials of the imagination (the 'irrational', the 'subconscious' etc. become, in his theory, synonymous with 'the imagination') and not simply receive what is already known or seen and make affecting shapes out of it. It is an intuitive act of discovery. His movement has, he says, broken with both 'ideas' and 'things', with the direct statement, the moral dialogue or parable, with realistic description, with innuendo, irony, anecdote and so on; these are the tools of practical men—they are legs, certainly, but poetry needs wings.

Like so many of their Chinese models, the Sixties' poets are sick of trying to succeed at Court, literally bored by the antitheses of political debate. It is a revolutionary transformation of human motives that they are after, a release of imaginative energy. Meantime they would as soon yield into their dreamworlds and offer 'Poems written out of laziness and silence' (the subtitle of their volume). Traditional forms and the rationalistic assumptions about experience which these seem to enact are abandoned for a cadenced *vers libre* (and it ought to be said that both Bly and Wright have achieved a more flexible and sustained speech line than seems available to the short-winded disciples of Charles Olson—for all the tedious theorizing on the subject which these poets have gone in for). By working at translations of foreign poets (the Sixties Press has brought out versions of Trakl, Jimenez, Vallejo, Neruda and others —imitations, really, I'm told), poets whose 'surrealism' they feel to have been neglected in America for the more planned out French variety, they predict a whole new area of possibilities for American poetry, and even that, via Spain, a style can be achieved which is common to both North and South America.

It seems to me that there are very real dangers that this movement will generate a cult of arbitrariness, of what Pound called 'any decayed cabbage cast upon any pale satin sofa'. The poems of Wright and Bly which most faithfully reflect the 'irrationalism' on which their theory seems so centrally based are, in fact, their least interesting; what really matters in their work, and there is a good deal that does, is misrepresented by the terms of Bly's propaganda. Here, for instance, is a first-rate poem by Wright, 'Eisenhower's visit to Franco, 1959'. I quote it in full:

> *The American hero must triumph over*
> *The forces of darkness,*
> *He has flown through the very light of heaven*

And come down in the slow dusk
Of Spain.

Franco stands in a shining circle of police.
His arms open in welcome.
He promises all dark things
Will be hunted down.

State police yawn in the prisons.
Antonio Machado follows the moon
Down a road of white dust,
To a cave of silent children
Under the Pyrenees.
Wine darkens in stone jars in villages.
Wine sleeps in the mouths of old men, it is
        a dark red color.

Smiles glitter in Madrid.
Eisenhower has touched hands with Franco, embracing
In a glare of photographers.
Clean new bombers from America muffle their engines
And glide down now.

Their wings shine in the searchlights
Of bare fields
In Spain.

To be sure, this is no slick anti-Fascist 'commentary'; nor is it a
mere subconscious event. Its reference is to an available historical
situation; its stance is personal, it proves what it proposes. The poem
has an almost spectral intensity, and Wright has buried his craft. The
images of 'light' and 'dark' which run in opposition throughout are
deployed with an impressive authority and tact. The shining circle of
police, the glittering smiles, the glare of photographers, the clean
bombers, the shining wings, the searchlights are invested with a
lethal metallic or hygienic purity; the purity of the brutal, the effi-
cient. They proceed from the light of a rhetorical heaven, and their

glamorous ritual threatens that 'all dark things will be hunted down'.
The ironic play upon the traditional associations of 'light' and 'dark'
is a crucial aspect of the poem's method; the moon that Machado
follows and the white dust on the road propose an order of imaginative enlightenment which is in accord with the 'dark red color' of
the wine, not opposed to it in the rhetorical sin/virtue antithesis that
Franco and the forces of cerebral cleansing dispense. The tragically
immeasurable gulf between rhetoric and experience, ritual and
mystery, is perfectly enacted by the final image and the sombrely
declining cadences in which it is spoken. There is none of the predictable acidity or spleen of the orthodox progressive in this poem,
there is no point-making or underscoring. The image is permitted
to come forward but, and this is the point, it comes by way of discrimination, it makes energizing contact with the 'outer world'.
There are a number of poems from the Sixties Press movement
which do just this; one thinks particularly of Wright's 'Lying in a
Hammock at William Duffy's Farm', his President Harding poem,
Louis Simpson's 'Walt Whitman at Bear Mountain', Robert Bly's
'Condition of the Working Classes', and there are others. They are
original and relevant and they ought to be read.

But when Donald Hall, in his introduction to the Penguin *Contemporary American Poetry*, talks of this 'new imagination' which
'reveals through images a subjective life which is *general*' he is, I
think, pointing out a real danger which these poets have too rarely
recognized. In their best poems, the correspondences that are revealed may seem extravagant at times (and after *New Lines Two*,
with its 'cardinal English virtues', we could all use some extravagance) but they are finally verifiable and coherent; the parts from
which their highly personal 'new wholes' are created can be seen to
derive from shared concrete experience:

> *In a field of sunlight between two pines,*
> *The droppings of last year's horses*
> *Blaze up into golden stones.*
> *I lean back, as the even darkens and comes on.*

> *A chicken hawk floats over, looking for home.*
> *I have wasted my life.*

This is in direct and admirable descent from *Prufrock*, with its foggy cat. But the poetry which most closely follows Bly's theory of the released subconscious, which is anti-metaphoric in the sense that it seeks to sever the Image from all referential burdens, is surely doomed to either generalities or eccentricities. To particularize without disclosing the terms on which one particular has been chosen rather than any other is to court triviality; to avoid this, and yet still to keep out of the objective world, is to lapse into primary abstractions or Sitwellian evocatives, it is to invite the reader to populate your rockery with his own favourite brand of gnomes:

> *There is this cave*
> *In the air behind my body*
> *That nobody is going to touch:*
> *A cloister, a silence*
> *Closing around a blossom of fire.*
> *When I stand upright in the wind,*
> *My bones turn to dark emeralds.*

If this is a riddle, one can think of some fairly vulgar solutions; it is so thinly fanciful, the key words could be permutated or replaced by a dozen others of approximate sense. It fails precisely because of its inwardness.

Setting aside the 'public' poems which I have mentioned, one is finally conscious of the narrow range of imagery in which these poets work. Snow, leaves, jewels, grass, silent woods, sudden movements of gentle animals (cf. Trakl), minimal alterations of the face of nature—these recur obsessively (or *perhaps*, to be charitable, by some esoteric plot) and they are asked to sustain far too incalculable a weight of significance. There is an absence of other people that makes a reiterated identification with the experience of deers seem paltry or sentimental. Colin Falck has called the manner dangerously parodiable, and he is right—parody usually succeeds self-parody.

There is something insidious about the speechless approval with
which certain American reviewers have greeted the Sixties Press
activities—it is the response that Bly's propaganda demands, and it
is at the same level a guilty response, after all those years of enslavement under Brooks-and-Warren. But penance may be done at the
expense of genuine achievement; some of these poems are better
than others and there are still, however approximate, ways of
judging. Louis Simpson, in the Spring 1963 *Hudson Review*, wel-
comed Bly's book, *Silence in the Snowy Fields*, like this: 'There has
been very little poetry in English that represents states of being.
Wordsworth's is the only great poetry in English to have done so.
Mr. Bly in his poems shows states of being.' A year earlier, though,
he was more convincing:

> *Yesterday I met Thomas.*
> *He was wearing a cloak and smoking marijuana,*
> *and in his hip pocket he carried a volume*
> *of Pablo Neruda.*
> *'What is this, Thomas?' I said.*
> *'Are you going to a masquerade?'*
>
> *'I have cast off my old ways' he answered,*
> *'and I advise you to do the same.*
> *It is all testicles nowadays and light,*
> *and a series of ecstatic exclamations.'*
> *Whereon he struck his guitar*
> *which he produced from his brief case*
> *and began to sing of various mountains*
> *in Chile. The stars figured prominently*
> *and there was talk of the full testicles of the night.*
> *'Thomas', I said, 'is this the new poetry?'*
> *'It is the new world', he replied.*
> *This kind of answer always leaves me feeling foolish.*

1964

The Making of the Movement

When the anthology *New Lines* appeared in 1956, the ground had more than been prepared; it had been practically churned into a quagmire. The advance promotion had in fact been initiated two years earlier, in the *Spectator*, with Anthony Hartley declaring to the world (in an unsigned leading article) that there existed a group of young poets who were ripe to dislodge the old forties gang. 'For better or worse', he wrote, 'we are now in the presence of the only considerable movement in English poetry since the Thirties.' These young poets (few of them were named, but they included the newly famous—as novelists—Kingsley Amis and John Wain, both of them regular *Spectator* reviewers) were announced to be in concerted reaction against the tangled and pretentious neo-romanticism of the post-war years; where the old lot had been bardic, overblown and religiose, these new men were clever, cagey, scornful. They had re-discovered irony, wit and syntax, they bowed the knee to Leavis, Empson and Orwell. More than all this, though, they represented in their verse moral attitudes which were excitingly appropriate to the grey new Britain of the fifties. Coining the title by which the group came to be officially identified, Hartley went on to draw a swift identi-kit portrait of 'The Movement':

> It is bored by the despair of the Forties, not much interested in suffering, and extremely impatient of poetic sensibility, especially poetic sensibility about 'the writer and society'. So it's goodbye to all those rather sad little discussions about 'how the writer ought to live' and it's goodbye to the Little Magazine and 'experimental writing'. The Movement, as well as being anti-phoney, is anti-wet; sceptical, robust, ironic, prepared to be as comfortable

as possible in a wicked, commercial, threatened world which doesn't look, anyway, as if it's going to be changed much by a couple of handfuls of young English writers.

The odd thing about Hartley's communiqué (aside from the fact that the poets in question, though assertedly fairly numerous, had published only a few pamphlets and one or two small press hardbacks) was the transparently calculated tone in which it was delivered; the tone, pushing and unblushing, of the hard sell. Readers at the time must have felt a bit puzzled and bullied; the material itself (which Hartley obtrusively avoided discussing in any detail) seemed so thin and elusive, the claims made for it so strident. And those who had not yet got round to reading *Lucky Jim* would hardly have felt tempted by the flaunted philistinism. Those who had read *Lucky Jim*, of course, might well have detected a highbrow-debunking hoax; let's show them how easy it is to start one of their phoney trends.

In the weeks following the *Spectator*'s P.R. job, there were some sardonic rejoinders from, as it were, the battle-front: Alan Brownjohn and Anthony Thwaite (both at the time editing Oxford poetry magazines in which some of the supposed Movementeers were often to be found) wrote deflating letters, with Thwaite ironically acknowledging that the article had 'the importance of a white paper in a field where previous remarks merely had the nature of, say, interdepartmental memoranda'. But the poets actually named by Hartley held their peace, and throughout the ensuing chat they tacitly collaborated in the construction and promotion of their group identity —though at the same time quietly murmuring that the whole thing was a bit absurd. 'We ridiculed and deprecated "the Movement" even as we kept it going,' Donald Davie has confessed:

All of us in the Movement had read the articles in *Scrutiny* about how the reputations of Auden and Spender and Day Lewis were made by skilful promotion and publicity and it was to placate *Scrutiny* readers that we pretended (and sometimes deceived ourselves as well as others) that the Movement was not being 'sold' to the public in the same way; that John Wain on the BBC and later

I

Bob Conquest with his anthology *New Lines* weren't just touching the pitch with which we others wouldn't be defiled. Again, I
limit myself to my own case; I remember nothing so distastefully
as the maidenly shudders with which I wished to know nothing
of the machinery of publicity even as I liked publicity and profited
from it.

Davie is perhaps right to feel anguished, and there is no doubt that
the Movement, along with the Sitwells, has its distinctive niche in
the history of publicity—it was a take-over bid and it brilliantly
succeeded. Indeed, by the time *New Lines* actually came out (it had
been preceded, in 1955, by D. J. Enright's *Poets of the 1950s*—but
this was published in Japan and wasn't much noticed) it had evidently succeeded all too well. Almost every young university poet
had become a Movementeer; the Oxford and Cambridge magazines, the Fantasy Press pamphlets, the column-ends of many of the
weeklies, were brimming over with neatly tailored ironies, with
feeble neo-Augustan posturings and effortful Empsonian pastiche.
The talentless had been given a verse-recipe only slightly more difficult to follow than that handed out by Tambimuttu fifteen years
earlier.

The task of *New Lines* was not to inaugurate a Movement, but to
stop the rot by sifting the senior members from the mass of imitators
and disciples. D. J. Enright's anthology had already made it clear
that these seniors—Amis, Wain, Davie, John Holloway, Philip
Larkin, Robert Conquest and Elizabeth Jennings—were most of
them already fairly gloomy about the fashion they'd precipitated.
John Wain wrote:

> I am, in fact, sometimes told that an article on the poetry of
> Empson which I contributed to the final issue of Penguin *New
> Writing* (1950) was responsible for starting the astonishing vogue
> of his poetry which has produced so many diminutive Empsons
> in the last five years. If so, I have certainly a grave charge to
> answer.

The others spoke of 'too much value being attached to intellectuality', of 'well constructed dry bones among the younger poets',

of a verse 'too limited in its scope, insufficiently various and adven-
turous', of the prevailing aridity, academicism and triviality. Of
course, these reservations were delicately balanced by acknow-
ledgements that, bad as it was, the new stuff was much preferable to
the work it had supplanted (and it does not take a subtle eye to detect
the essential boastfulness of Wain's self-deprecations).

One's suspicion that a principal function of New Lines was to
annex for its participants a pigeon-hole in literary history which was
beginning to get over-crowded is supported by Kingsley Amis's
testimony in the Enright book. He writes: 'nobody wants any more
poems about philosophers or paintings or novelists or art galleries or
mythology or foreign cities or other poems'. I have heard this statement quoted as one of the Movement's rallying cries; in fact it is
more like a death warrant. Amis accurately describes here the subject matter of most of the poems in New Lines—just under half the
poems in the book, for instance, are to do with poetry, painting or
foreign cities, and most of the others are heavily sprinkled with
Merlins and Spinozas. A neat ruse, to kill off the Movement even as
you are about to foster its historical significance.

Robert Conquest's introduction to the book itself adopts a similar
strategy. In modest tones it outlines the well-known virtues of
clarity, honesty, intelligence and rigorous empiricism, but notes
with sadness that 'any forthright lead will find its followers and
imitators among young writers' and that a number of young poets
are 'following Empsonian and similar academic principles and often
producing verse of notable aridity'.

Today, looking back on the poets included in New Lines (the
Enright team, plus Thom Gunn) it seems difficult to conceive of
aridity more notable than theirs. It is difficult, also, to fathom how
such largely tame and awkward verses could ever have been found
dazzlingly fresh and skilful. The intellectual brilliance of Elizabeth
Jennings, for example, consists of a laborious obsession with 'the
mind'. 'This afternoon disturbs within the mind', 'And this aware-
ness grows upon itself, Fastens on minds', 'Image and pattern com-
bined into a whole/Pattern within the loving mind', 'But when the

music ends/There lie within our minds/Thoughts that refuse to fit',
'As thought to unfasten from the mind/Our moods and give them
outward forms', 'There is so much/That separates those motionless
proud horses/From minds that only move through words'. And
these are selected from a mere ten poems. Miss Jennings's weakly
ruminative verses are stiffened with some neat travel views, but she
is no more rigorous and complicated than, say, Bernard Spencer.
Similarly, John Holloway's contorted cerebrations, though certainly arid and technically ingenious, are no more demanding than
Roy Fuller. And neither in Holloway's work nor in the heavily
abstract soliloquies of Robert Conquest is there any sense of the
poems' supposed formal skills being any more than fiddlingly external to what is being argued and thought out. Much the same could
be said of Thom Gunn's contributions (in large sections much more
strangulated and cumbersome than anything in the book) but here
one has to concede a novelty of tone and *persona*; a *persona*, however,
utterly at odds with ideals of moderation or ordinariness. One
doubts that Gunn had learned anything, at this stage, from any
modern poet.

An anthology including Miss Jennings, Holloway, Conquest,
Enright, and Thom Gunn would hardly have attracted any group
label; such a volume could also have offered work by Spencer,
Fuller and Henry Reed and no one would have thought it odd. Indeed, Henry Reed would probably have been considered closer to
the regulation Movementeer than any of the others. The anthology's
real claim to notoriety resides, appropriately enough, in the handful
of poems which self-consciously seek such notoriety; those poems,
in other words, which speak directly from and about the literary
milieu of the early fifties. They are poems-as-criticism, or as literary
journalism. Amis's 'Against Romanticism', 'Wrong Words',
'Something Nasty in the Bookshop', 'Here is Where', Davie's
'Rejoinder to a Critic', 'Cherry Ripe', 'Too Late for Satire', 'Re-
membering the Thirties', Wain's 'Reason for Not Writing Nature
Poetry', 'Who Speaks My Language' and 'Eighth Type of Ambiguity': all are mini-polemics against the standard romantic postures

of the late forties. They are prescriptions for the new poetry, and to that extent are enactments of it, but each is saturated with a strategic, blow-striking self-awareness, each inhabits an imaginative world dominated by trivial exigencies of literary warfare.

Efforts, in some of these poems, to extend a narrowly literary anti-romanticism into a general critique of what Conquest describes as 'great systems of theoretical constructs' or 'agglomerations of unconscious commands' now look fairly laborious and crude. The real spur, the true source of the wit, the edge, the slangy confidence of the best Movement poems, was thoroughly ephemeral. The Movement, in fact, could almost be said to have been the sum of its manifestos; its most apt footnote can be found in Anthony Hartley's *Spectator* review of *New Lines*, in which the erstwhile prophet is to be heard calling for 'a reversion to dynamic romanticism'.

Conspicuously absent from the foregoing 'reappraisal' is any comment on the one poet whose contribution to *New Lines* seems to me to have any lasting potency; at one level, it could be said that Philip Larkin's poems provide an exact model for what the Movement was supposed to be seeking. But having noted his lucidity, his debunkery, his technical accomplishment and other such 'typical' attributes, one would still be left with the different and deeper task of describing the quality of his peculiar genius, the task of talking about poems rather than postures.

1971

Philip Larkin

The publication of Philip Larkin's third book, *The Whitsun Weddings*, was awaited with genuine eagerness, by his enemies as well as his friends. In many ways it was an advance on *The Less Deceived*. That volume was generally agreed to be skilful and perceptive, to achieve nearly all that it seems to aim at, but the quarrel with Larkin has rarely been over individual poems which can be exposed as failures on their own terms—it has usually amounted to a total questioning of his narrow range of rather negative attitudes. He has been variously accused of provincialism, of arid reticence, of nourishing his sense of defeat to the point of fascinated self-parody.

Now it is certainly true that a poetry like his, which is aimed to expose a core of personal vacuity, of lapsed resentment at opportunities missed, privileges withheld and so on, will invariably run risks of this kind, always threatening to spread out into what will appear a desiccated self-regard. It was perhaps in order to counter such impressions that Larkin very often assumed the offhand, debunking stance that is so familiar in his earlier volume; a stance which generally has the effect of diffusing his personal predicament into an inclusive and unconvincing sneer at the Emotional Life (at 'Sex, yes, but what is sex?'), ranking it along with God and Art as just another tarnished absolute, a snare of affectation. Larkin to some extent gets round the unevenness of tone that must arise from this by projecting a *persona* who is seen to actively relish his impoverishment as 'undeceived', a mark of superiority over the herd. At the same time, of course, we are made to know that the poet sees through the rationalization he is promoting.

Very often Larkin's punchline will suggest a whole range of emotional possibilities which the rest of his poem has been careful to ignore. For instance, in the last lines of 'Poetry of Departures' the phrase 'a life reprehensibly perfect' not only completes the cycle of rather smug self-imprisonment which the poem has been plotting but also introduces a whole new dimension, of despair. The tongue is removed from the cheek and is given a sharp bite. This is the kind of thing, too, that happens in 'Church Going', where the final recognition of the church as a 'serious house on serious earth' is not so much a natural intensification of the irreverent early stanzas as a lofty rejection of their slick disengagement. It is almost as if the *persona* is being scolded by the poet.

The best poems in *The Less Deceived* are those like 'At Grass' where the poet has none of these problems of attitude but discovers an objective situation that can dramatize his sense of exclusion and defeat, or those like 'Next Please' where he attempts a kind of representative wisdom and operates from a rhetorical 'we'. Here his skill at maintaining a complex reflection through several elegant stanzas without cramping either his syntax or his natural speech movement is really remarkable. One can think of few contemporary poets who can manage this kind of writing without stuttering into the pompous or obvious. In Larkin, though, it seems effortless.

In *The Whitsun Weddings* volume Larkin allows these metaphoric and reflective gifts more scope than he did in *The Less Deceived*. Only now and then—in poems like 'Self's the Man' and 'A Study of Reading Habits', for example—does one discover the old self-deprecatory habit and in these it is handled with a light-hearted assertiveness that seems to signal the level on which it is meant to be taken. Larkin's sense of pity is now extended to the 'cut-price crowd' with their manipulated desires and their shoddy festivals, and to individuals like Mr. Bleaney, from whom love has been withheld, or the widow in 'Love Songs in Age' whom it has cheated by promising to 'solve and satisfy/and set unchangeably in order'. Though Larkin is fairly caustic at the expense of that 'much-mentioned brilliance, love' and regularly discovers a pathos in the situation of those who have succumbed to it, his portrait of the loveless Mr. Bleaney is one of his most compelling. There is a sense in which Larkin's ubiquitous compassion tends to reduce people to the sum of their paraphernalia, but in this poem his observation and selection of detail is rigorous enough for this to be acceptable—Bleaney's tragedy is that he probably *can* be summed up in this way, by his flowered curtains, his saucer-souvenir, his four aways. The last two stanzas are expertly managed. They work into a suspended knottiness that is beautifully resolved by the poet's final intervention. It has not, we realize, been idle speculation—if the poet doesn't know about Bleaney, he does know about himself. The identification is chillingly complete. Bleaney is in his coffin and the poet has inherited his 'hired box':

> But if he stood and watched the frigid wind
> Tousling the clouds, lay on the fusty bed
> Telling himself that this was home, and grinned
> And shivered, without shaking off the dread
>
> That how we live measures our own nature,
> And at his age having no more to show
> Than one hired box should make him pretty sure
> He warranted no better, I don't know.

But how might Bleaney have improved his situation? Not, from what we are told in other parts of the book, by reading, travel or marriage. Money? We never learn, in the title poem, if having the real thing instead of 'jewellery substitutes' would have helped. In 'Faith Healer' the suggestion seems to be that there is no getting away from that 'much-mentioned brilliance':

> in everyone there sleeps
> A sense of life lived according to love.
> To some it means the difference they could make
> By loving others, but across most it sweeps
> As all they might have done had they been loved.

This moving ambiguity runs throughout. On the one hand, there is

'everyone making love and going shares', love that is organized into
the drudgery of marriage, that cheats and disappoints and is dis-
proved by time. On the other, there is the isolation and discontent
of those who have never had it, or who, rejecting it on these terms,
seek it instead as 'an enormous yes' that can be intimated as force-
fully by a pair of 'new, slightly out-moded shoes' as it can by
'wheat's restless silence'. The closing lines of the title-poem seem to
contain and energize this conflict. The arrow shower is both ironic
and visionary and being so can beautifully concentrate the strands
of aspiration and defeat which are present in the dramatic commentary of which it is the superb climax:

> *and it was nearly done, this frail*
> *Travelling coincidence; and what it held*
> *Stood ready to be loosed with all the power*
> *That being changed can give. We slowed again,*
> *And as the tightened brakes took hold, there swelled*
> *A sense of falling, like an arrow shower*
> *Sent out of sight, somewhere becoming rain.*

Larkin is not always as skilful as he is here. He often delivers some
terrible rhymes (easiest/honest/unrest/; lines/limousines etc.) and
breaks his lines against the speech rhythm to achieve them, as in
'Sunny Prestatyn', where—in search of rhymes for 'sand' and 'poster'
—he does this

> *Behind her, a hunk of coast, a*
> *Hotel with palms*
> *Seemed to expand from her thighs and*
> *Spread breast-lifting arms.*

He can also lapse into a rollicking Betjemanesque which does not
suit him; though the worst example occurs in the second stanza of
'The Large Cool Store', which is, anyway, a rather silly poem
about nighties.

On the whole, though, one can only welcome and admire this
volume. It has all the virtues of *The Less Deceived* and very few of

its faults. Larkin has extended his range of interests with admirable ease and seems no longer concerned to pose. There is no saying what he might go on to achieve.

1964

Donald Davie

Donald Davie's *Events and Wisdoms* is his first collection since *A Winter Talent* (1957)—though he has published two long works in the meantime—and is a scrupulous report on his 'auspiciously begun/ Adventure of blessing the world', on the new models and objectives which he has been selecting and shaping over the past few years. In the past Davie has often given the impression of being rather too wise for the event, too tidily burdened by his professional tasks and trials, too elegantly armed against reviewer's repartee—very little seemed to break free from mere programmatic attitude to assume an independent poetic self-assurance, and there was always something bogus and forced about his moralizing anti-romanticism. *Events and Wisdoms* has the usual air of being written to a theory—but it is a rather better theory and Davie is no longer content simply to decorate his ideas or cleverly expound them; he is now prepared to demonstrate what he means.

In *A Winter Talent* it was his refusal to push far beyond theory that fitted him for Frank Kermode's title of 'iron-lung poet'; he devoted considerable intelligence and skill to the problems of breathing yet was never able to get up and do it naturally. It was too deliberately a rejoinder to the romantic critic; excess of feeling had not only impurified our diction and corroded our syntax, it had precipitated all that was loathsome in our recent history and fraudulent in our personal relations. It is on these grounds that Davie flourishes his neutral tone and strikes his aggressively decorous pose; better to be 'a pasticheur of late Augustan styles', he insists, than one of those 'quick bright talents' that 'burn their boats continually' (more 'Lines for a Book'?). The formal arrangement, the honourable reserve; these are the virtues and Davie parades them time and again. Rarely, though, do they seem to be achieved as the difficult prize; they are ready to hand and dispensed with a dry, nagging facility.

Not understanding people is also a matter for self-congratulation; there is, certainly, 'a lean young housewife' 'with the glance I like to think that I can recognize' and here and there a generalization about, say, those inflexibles who never show their hand until compelled; but on the whole it is rare that Davie finds himself 'liking to think I feel these sympathies'. He prefers to present himself as chilled, pre-occupied, a wintry talent; even so, there can be a certain unbending pathos in his encounters with the adversary:

> *You warm to me. I thaw, and am approved.*
> *But, to be frank, the sentiment is forced.*
> *When I pretend, for your sake, to be moved.*
>
> *You might have moved, you never shall persuade.*
> *You grow too warm. I must be moving on.*

Of course, 'You grow too warm' barely conceals its self-criticism, but, as with the play on 'move', it is rather fun getting it all these ways at once.

Artists are frequently invoked and those who are not artists are treated either as if they were (for instance, in 'Obiter Dicta', the poet sees his father as the representative of a generation fond of 'Great Truths', prone to 'afflatus', searching for wisdom where we are pleased to detect ironies), or, more successfully, as if they were made by artists. 'The Mushroom Gatherers' is the best poem in *A Winter Talent*; Davie dramatizes his ideal by first acknowledging its other-worldliness, that it is a mystery that he has imagined. His 'strange walkers' are immune 'from human ills, crestfallen and serene' and move with a 'strange decorum'; they descend from the essential Romantic vision of an immortalized mortality that is revealed to the guilt-ridden poet in Keats's *Fall of Hyperion*, and they have their remote, spectral counterparts in early Pound and the pre-Raphaelites.

Significantly, though, Davie presents them as 'after Mickiewicz'; translation, or 'imitation', not only provides Davie with the kind of subject which his knowing habit will not allow him to treat directly, it also makes available to him—in a manageable, distanced form— the passions whose disruptive energy he explicitly fears but oddly seems to yearn for in his personal poetry:

> *No ripening curve can be allowed to sag*
> *On cubist's canvas or in sculptor's stone;*
> *Informal fruit, that burgeons from the swag,*
> *Would spoil the ripening that is art's alone.*
> *This can be done with cherries. Other fruit*
> *Have too much bloom of import, like the grape,*
> *Whose opulence comes welling from a root*
> *Struck far too deep to yield so pure a shape.*

Of course, Davie is sharp enough to see that it is a measure of his narrowness that he should want to pretend this to be true; but the pretence is for him a necessary one, and it is our appreciation of its necessity that gives the book what depth and edge it has. Beneath the mannered, crafty surface of *A Winter Talent* one can intermittently sense the puzzled dialogue of a writer who feels it his burden to be mannered and crafty, to make his Art proof not only against philistinism but also against the pandering excesses of anti-philistinism; the suspicion that in assuming this burden he may be avoiding others is inescapable, and it accounts for a good deal of Davie's early attitudinizing.

But there was enough seriousness there to guarantee development; Davie has invariably been his own most acute critic. He has condemned the 'craven defensiveness' of his early manner, his readiness to woo a highbrow élite, and in particular he has attacked the absence in all Movement poetry 'of outward and non-human things apprehended crisply for their own sakes'. In recent years he has followed Williams and Olson in campaigning against the narrow anthropomorphism of the contemporary poet, his vain imprisonment within an unfurnished personal reality. He has predicted that 'we may be in for a revival of nature poetry, or at least of a poetry which is as much about things as about people'. In the service of this aim he has developed the notion of analogies between the arts; just as in stressing the syntactical structure of the poem he was seeing poetry as music, so in insisting upon humility before the natural object he is seeing poetry as sculpture (but not, he says, 'sculpture as model-ling' which will lead the poet into the 'overweening presumption' that he can make 'nature serve him'; rather 'sculpture as carving' where he is seen to be 'the servant of nature').

Davie is ever the moralist, though; his neutral tone was not just a literary strategy, it was a moral necessity. In the same way, his con-templation of the non-human—'realizing this stone wall as different from all other stone walls'—is defended in terms of its moral in-structiveness; it can afford a 'model which you can then apply to human relations'. Thus in *Events and Wisdoms*, Davie not only sets out to write landscape poetry, he also takes the landscape image and its treatment by the human eye, time and the weather as a figure for poetry itself; it is against the messy, irritated flux of human be-haviour that he opposes his sculptured stone, not just as a 'type of ideal virtue' but as an affirmation of art. The stress cuts deeper when he considers his own interfering relationship with what he sees, believing with Pasternak that the artist has not 'invented metaphor but discovered it in nature and reproduced it faithfully'; the effort involves withstanding the distractions not just of one's neuroses but also of one's knowledge. It is this kind of effort that persistently pre-occupies Davie in the first section of the book, and one has to bear with a good deal of muttering

> No I must feed myself
> On feelings fresh from their source.

> It is Breughel, or Samuel Palmer
> Some painter, coming between
> My eye and the truth of a farmer.

The landscape and the 'so uncreative' weather that threatens and alters it remain fairly inert, cluttered with disappointed soliloquiz-ing; one gets slightly weary of being told how hard it is to write

about this sort of thing and in the absence of much really strong
observation one begins to suspect that nature is after all being violated, however subtly, to serve the poet's self-absorbed humility. A
rat oughtn't to be 'sleek and lissom', nor should a river be 'like a
snake' in such a dedicated enterprise. Only in 'Across the Bay', the
excellent poem that closes his first section, does Davie come near to
an inclusive orchestration of his various themes; here his familiar
confrontations are enlivened by a direct warmth of feeling as well as
an arresting eye; the human interrupts and measures the non-
human as Art stumbles against Life:

> The beach so-called was a blinding splinter of limestone,
> A quarry outraged by hulls.
> We took pleasure in that; the emptiness, the hardness
> Of the light, the silence and the water's stillness.
>
> But it was the setting for one of our murderous scenes.
> This hurt and goes on hurting;
> The venomous soft jelly, the undersides.
> We could stand the world if it were hard all over.

It is in the second and third sections of the book that Davie's
adventure really seems to bear fruit (the fourth part, 'After an Accident' is an attempt at intimacy but is prosy and awkward; to this
extent, Davie really needs his theory—one cannot easily imagine
him writing a successful love poem. 'You had to nearly die/For me
to know I lived', the punch-line of this sequence, is all attitude, and
typical). In the middle sections, Davie takes Lowell's *Life Studies* as
his model; he eliminates commentary and speculation and trusts in
the expressive relations between his concrete effects. The result is a
new richness of phrasing and a general toughening of the total
structure of each poem; throughout, too, there is a sense of release
at the sudden availability of the concrete world and very little is
faked in his terse piling up of correspondences. The debt to Lowell
is considerable; at times, disturbingly direct. For instance, the
brandishing of proper names and of historical and geographical

peculiarities can get tiresome and Lowell's trick of handing out three
sharp adjectives at a time, though brilliantly done in the original, is
not easily borrowed; 'clammy, electric, torrid', 'empty, unwatered,
crumbling'. Nevertheless, there is enough distinct achievement here
for one to welcome Lowell as a general influence; in poems like
'Agave in the West', 'A Christening', and 'In California', Davie is
impressively in control and, at last, both wise and eventful:

> *The new baby is fed.*
> *I stumble back to bed.*
> *I hear the owls for a long time*
>
> *Hunting. Or are they never*
> *In the winter grey of before dawn,*
> *Those pure long quavers,*
>
> *Cries of love? I put my arms around you.*
> *Small mice freeze among tussocks.*
> *The baby wails in the next room.*
>
> *Upstairs Mrs. Ramsden*
> *Dies, and the house*
> *Is full of the cries of the newborn*

1964

Lives and Letters

WALLACE STEVENS
Letters of Wallace Stevens selected and edited by Holly
Stevens

When Wallace Stevens died in 1955, *The Times* noted with a mild
surprise that his entry in the American *Who's Who* began: 'Stevens,
Wallace, insurance . . .' The memory of Dylan Thomas was still
poignant (though Stevens himself had refused to speak at a memorial
meeting: 'He spent what little money he made without regard to
his responsibilities') and it was not yet fashionable for poets to present themselves as knock-me-down sales representatives of verse.
The chap next door might sell insurance, he might even write poetry,
but surely nobody did both—at least not well. Stevens did, and got
irritated with those who thought it odd. He sold insurance at least
as efficiently as he wrote poetry, and in both areas he stuck single-
mindedly to the one job, getting slicker at it all the time.

He joined the Hartford Accident and Indemnity Company in
1916, and simply stayed put, placidly working his way up to a vice-
presidency in 1934. For nearly forty years he lived in the same town,
attended the same office. And before that, he had done nothing un-
toward. He went to Harvard, tried his hand at journalism, gave that
up for law school, was admitted to the Bar in 1904. A period of
general practice paved the way for his long stay in Hartford. He
married wisely, he never made 'that million dollars I started out to
make'. Though he loved things foreign and exotic, he hardly ever
travelled; his business man's dream of the primitively lovely was fed
by working trips to Miami, and he got friends to send him tea and
carvings from the East, books and paintings from Europe. He
shunned the literary racket, though towards the end of his life he

rather enjoyed playing the grand old man, dispensing Bollingens and Guggenheims. He took up no political positions, but occasionally aired his changing prejudices; for example, 'I am pro-Mussolini personally' because 'the Italians have as much right to take Ethiopia from the coons as the coons had to take it from the boa-constrictors'. 'The misery that underlies fascism would probably be much vaster, much keener, under any other system . . .' (1935). Ten years after writing this, Stevens was refusing to contribute to a symposium on Ezra Pound's war record on the grounds that even geniuses are 'subject to the common disciplines'.

Where, in Stevens's grimly ordered life, did poetry fit in? In a curious way, it didn't fit in at all, except as a kind of necessary prop or dignified retreat. Since one of the purposes of Stevens's painstaking effort towards a supreme fiction was to tell us, by example, how to quicken and illuminate the dull mass of the ordinary, we can hardly blame him for having avoided a sensational biography, or for having written letters of common sense and cautious sentiment but of very faint dramatic impact. 'The sea is loveliest far in the abstract when the imagination can feed upon the idea of it. The thing itself is dirty, wobbly and wet.' This is the kind of thing one must expect to show itself more tediously in the letters than in the poetry, since poetry is the only way of justifying such arrogance. But it also suggests, or seems to, the way in which Stevens came to regard his own daily life, and how he managed to survive it for so long. The huge discrepancy between 'real life' and the 'life of the imagination' was more than just a theory that he played around with, or derived from the accident of his own poetic practice; it was a solid, experienced fact about the kind of life he led. The imagination was more marvellous than the materials it had to work on, than 'the thing itself'; the more protected and uneventful the actual business of living could be made, the more magnificent the flight from it must seem.

To have limited the imagination to a merely revelatory role not only would have involved suppressing its superb inventiveness, it would also have obliged the poet to live a much more interesting—

or, in Stevens's likely view, a more messily complicated—life than he had nerve, or need, for. As a young man, Stevens had a rural hide-out he could escape to from New York; it was fine until he found some eggshells littering the ground: 'sure sign of a man + his wife + a child or two, loafing in my temple. How fine, though, was the mystery of everything except the damned eggshells.' Eliminating the human intruder—'confusing beyond measure'—was for Stevens almost a matter of conscious policy; and there is throughout his letters an icily discouraging aloofness that permits no end of formal, friendly discourse about poetry, but forbids—even with his long-standing correspondents—any real attempt at intimacy. Stevens met very few of the people he most enjoyed writing to, and only a hand-ful got on to Christian-name terms with him. That the majority of his letters were dictated to a secretary may in part account for the general coolness, but then why did he dictate them?

Apart from a few early letters to his wife (though most of these are cut to aphoristic snatches), one or two to his daughter and some bursts of misery in his old age, there is a desolating—but never de-solated—lack of deep involvement in the people Stevens is writing to; we all have our problems, is the frequent implication, just as we all have our fictions. There are ideas galore—but most of these are fairly familiar from his essays—and lots of gay and earnest exegesis of difficult poems; there are publishing difficulties, snippets of literary gossip, a passing craze for genealogy. But all utterly invul-nerable. There can be no doubt that this expertly edited, beautifully produced, volume has brought us that bit closer to the poems but it also has the strange effect of making 'Stevens, Wallace, in-surance . . .' seem even further out of range. Which is more or less where he wanted to be.

1967

RUPERT BROOKE
The Letters of Rupert Brooke edited by Geoffrey Keynes

Four years ago Christopher Hassall published a 500-page biography of Rupert Brooke. Now we have 700 pages of letters. Both tomes aim to persuade us that Brooke was more interesting than the 'Apollo golden-haired' business gave him credit for. Not more interesting as a poet, but as a person. Geoffrey Keynes concedes that Brooke was 'not a major poet, a great letter-writer or a mature personality', but would have us concede that he possessed 'exceptional personal attractions', an 'intellect of rare quality' and certain 'perceptive sensibilities'. And this was more or less Hassall's view. His courteous biography (which we now see to have been based almost exclusively on Brooke's own letters) presented Brooke as a comely young brilliant, immensely promising but never quite grown-up.

Brooke would have been delighted by such verdicts, just as he would have been thrilled by the manufactured and dismantled myths. And they are verdicts which need adding to rather than rebutting. From an early age Brooke had a cool eye on the biographies. (And Geoffrey Keynes seems from an even earlier age to have assumed his editorial responsibilities. He upbraids the beardless Brooke for not dating a letter and Brooke loftily retorts: 'if you are so concerned at the difficulty which will arise when that letter is included in the "Life and Letters" you might obviate it by dating the letters when you receive them'.) Brooke was a tireless poseur and one of his favourite roles was that of the doomed prodigy, the flawed beauty of vast promise and exquisite, slight achievement. At school when he was not winning prizes, parading with the O.T.C. or excelling on the playing fields, he nurtured an image of decadent malaise, of sweet, suicidal aestheticism. It was done with great imitative skill (he was deep in Wilde and Dowson) and with a measure of self-mockery, and it does not seem to have seriously interfered with his position as the housemaster's bright son. But it does seem to have answered some deep boredom in him: 'Do not be surprised to hear that I am found dead some day in the Close, a self-thrust dagger in my heart and a volume of Swinburne pallidly open before me. It may be the only way.' Brooke never really outgrew the adolescent death-wish, he simply found new 'adult' contexts for it. At Cambridge, where 'my present pose is as a socialist', he imagined himself 'dying fantastically upon some street barricade'. In love with Katherine Cox, he tortured her, and indulged himself, with repeated threats of suicide. Heading for war, he writes: 'I really think large numbers of male people don't want to die; which is odd.' And to John Drinkwater: 'Come and die. It'll be great fun.'

And this is the one constant element in all Brooke's roles. He was genuinely more afraid of growing old than of dying; there is no glamorous way of growing old. He formed a pact with some Cambridge friends that in 1933 they would meet on Basle Station, having kicked off their vile grown-up responsibilities, and would be young again: 'Suppose that a band of the splendid young people in the past had formed a scheme to escape the great destroyer, to continue young, and suppose they had succeeded—wouldn't that have been a *wonderful* and unequalled triumph? a splendid example for the world? and a glory for themselves?' The alternative was to become a 'greying literary hack, mumbling along in some London suburb'. Just as Brooke's idyllic trip to the South Seas was 'like getting back to childhood', so was his last trip to Constantinople: 'The eye grows clearer and the heart.'

In his relations with women Brooke seems also to have been seeking emotional asylum from the adult world. Evoking blissful prospects, he speaks mostly of laying his head in his beloved's lap, of having her run her fingers through his hair. Although patronizing on intellectual matters (he addresses all his women as 'child'), he invariably presents himself in passive, helpless aspect when he talks of love.

Christopher Hassall's biography was reticent (or perhaps Hassall simply did not know) on his affair with Katherine Cox, and Geoffrey Keynes prints fewer letters relating to this chapter of Brooke's life than are summarized or quoted by Hassall. Was it merely sexual frustration that drove Brooke to his 'breakdown' and was it merely sexual guilt that made him want to cast Ka off once he had won her? Why, after the affair is over, does he say, 'I can't ever marry her: because of the great evil she did me,' and: 'Oh, child, I know I've done you great wrong. What could I do? it was so difficult. You had driven me mad.'

How much of a pose was the famous breakdown? There is something unpleasantly histrionic about the letters that Brooke poured out from Cannes, where he was recuperating in his mother's care, and it is notable that when Katherine responds to his wild threats of suicide and says she is coming to him, he replied, by telegram: 'for heaven's sake don't come on account of me or my letters was mad and wicked other letters on way'. His fear was of a confrontation between Katherine and his mother (who knew nothing of her: how mad was the mad lover whose nurse did not know he was in love?): 'I felt the old helplessness before authority creeping over me.' Geoffrey Keynes omits the telegram and at least one important letter relating to this incident. He also omits what Hassall describes as the 'Cannes-like stream of letters' which followed Katherine's visit to Brooke's home in March 1912. It was her first, long-feared, meeting with Brooke's stern mother (who was even at this point in ignorance of the affair) and she left before the weekend was over.

This incident seems to mark the final break—from then on he was the solicitous, guilt-racked guardian of the women he had wronged. (He also enjoyed posing for some time as a man of broken mind—writing to Virginia Stephen at the height of his affair with Katherine, he is ready to scoff conspiratorially at Katherine's bear-like practicality; he and Virginia, colleagues in neurosis, saw things differently.) There is a subsequent letter, said by Hassall to have 'touched the lowest depths'. Hassall deemed it unnecessary to quote from such deep stuff 'at length' (he prints a brief, unilluminating extract) but Keynes does not seem to have printed any of it. The task of selecting the relevant (but relevant to what?) letters from a huge and repetitious correspondence like Brooke's cannot have been easy, but readers puzzled by Hassall's enigmatic account of the Katherine Cox episode (as D. J. Enright was, in a brilliant review of the biography) will presumably be looking to the letters for more, not less, information.

As well as the problem of selection, there has been—in spite of that schoolboy altercation—the problem of dating the letters. Keynes admits that he may have got some of them in the wrong order, and certainly his datings do not always coincide with Hassall's. So the future is obliged to bring us another 500-page biography, 700 further pages of Brooke's letters; the gaps will be filled, the questions answered, and we will finally be sure that none of it was really worth the trouble. The new myth, the myth of the *real* Brooke, is doing very nicely.

1968

HART CRANE
Voyager: A Life of Hart Crane by John Unterecker

This large book has been spoken of as the definitive biography of Hart Crane; nothing else, we are told, remains to be discovered about his brief and tortured life. In one sense, this is clearly true. Unterecker spent ten years sifting the available documentary evidence and went to considerable lengths to track down and interview all those still living who had anything to do with Crane. Allotting an average of twenty pages to each year of Crane's life, he has been able to provide virtually a day-by-day account of the poet's moods and movements, dull as many of these were. Gaps in the existing biographies have been convincingly filled and as a result some important misconceptions have been set right.

We will no longer, for instance, be able to see Crane's relations with his businessman father as a caricature clash between the poetic and the mercantile; C. A. Crane emerges from this account a good deal more sympathetically than he does from Philip Horton's *Life*, and we now know that, brilliant as that early biography still seems,

Horton relied over-trustingly on Crane's mother's view of things. Torn horribly throughout his life between his warring parents, Crane was forever taking sides with one of them against the other; but although his commitment to his mother was always the more passionate, it was his father he increasingly turned to as his own psychic weaknesses began to show themselves—and his father was often splendidly equal to his son's demands. 'Please, my dear father, do not make the present too hard,—too painful for one whose fatal weakness is to love two unfortunate people,' Crane would beg. There are some very moving letters here in which C. A. Crane, by nature wholly resistant to Hart's habits and ideas, is seen effortfully —but with immense earnestness and dignity—struggling to break free of prejudices which he can see are poisoning their friendship. Pathetically, he tries to view his own business achievements with the kind of scorn he hopes his son will warm to. Such efforts never worked, of course, and a few days later C.A. would once more be the heavy father: but they are genuinely noble while they last.

It is this kind of revelation that makes Unterecker's book of real value—and not merely because it sets the historical record straight. The key problem with Crane's poetry is to determine why, after the delicately scrupulous achievement of *White Buildings*, he chose to embark on a project so disastrously grandiose as *The Bridge*; why, with his deep and careful self-awareness, he plunged into a mode that would allow so little scope for his best gifts. Approaching this as a problem requires, of course, a largely negative estimate of Crane's pseudo-epic, and there is no real sign that Unterecker believes the work to be a failure. (Indeed, there is no sign that the scholar has strong critical views about any of Crane's poetry.) None the less, learning about Crane's true attitude towards his father, and towards his father's ideals of industriousness, self-help, professional success, and so on, does shade in one small corner of the total picture; Crane was continually having to, and indeed wanting to, persuade his father that being a poet was just as much a matter of hard grind as being a candy salesman. To be 'constructing' a poem, to be welding and riveting something 'architectural'—a guilt in

Crane might well have been assuaged by viewing his vocation in these terms.

In a similar way, the detailed chronology provided by Unterecker permits one to speculate about the effect on Crane's development of his long, and agonizing, wait for the publication of *White Buildings*. While Crane was touting the book around publishers and getting more and more disheartened about its prospects, many of his closest literary friends and supporters—and in particular Gorham Munson —were in Paris and were busy falling for Apollinaire and Dada. Crane's objections to the new fashion were vehement, but he cannot have been unmoved at the prospect of his own book seeming out of date before it had even appeared. Thus, one finds him deploring in Apollinaire a superficial gaiety and optimism about things urban and industrial and pleading for 'the real and lasting appeal' of 'sadness'. Early in the next year, though, with *White Buildings* still not accepted, he is writing—again to Munson—of his plans for *The Bridge*; 'the bridge' itself, he says, will symbolize 'our constructive future, our unique identity, in which is included also our scientific hopes and achievements of the future'. Without making too much of it, one wonders if there was not a spark of opportunism in Crane's sudden—and, in the poem, thoroughly unconvincing—surge of prophetic optimism.

Any true explanation of the way Crane's career went will have to go far beyond such small considerations into the sort of psychoanalytic speculation that Philip Horton is so good at and which Unterecker hardly attempts. We hear in this book about the drunken bouts, the homosexual promiscuity, the rages and the sulks for which Crane is already famous; boring and repetitive though they tend to become, Unterecker does not in the least exploit their glamour. But, on the other hand, he does not really get down to exploring their self-destructive sources, nor attempt to relate what was happening to the life with what was happening to the poems. He has—and let us, in the end, thank him for it—provided the materials on which such an endeavour will, one hopes, eventually be based.

1971

ROBERT FROST
The Years of Triumph 1915–1938 by Lawrance Thompson

By the spring of 1912, he was thirty-eight years old. He was
convinced that if ever he was to assert himself artistically with
success, he must find the time and place to be completely selfish.

The first volume of Lawrance Thompson's biography of Frost
traced the poet's life up to just beyond the drawing of this hardly
novel insight; to 1915, in fact, when the poet—having won himself
a minor reputation in England with the publication of his first book
—journeyed back to America hoping for a similar, if not surpassing,
triumph there. We had learned, in this first volume, of Frost's
morose, vindictive, often suicidal personality, of his profound vanities and inconsistencies. He had not spent those long pre-England
years contentedly mending walls and picking apples; at best, he had
merely played with the idea of farming. The literary ambitions
which had eventually found some sort of fulfilment in England has
been there all along and Frost had not borne their frustration lightly.
Indeed, according to Thompson, he had been deeply damaged by it.
Tasting the success he'd been starved òf for nearly twenty years,
Frost discovered in himself an unhealthy appetite for more.

It is the consequences of this discovery that provide the chief
theme of Thompson's second volume—the manipulations, the
subterfuges, the often ugly hypocrisies that Frost was guilty of in
his neurotic quest for the reassurances of praise and fame. It is a
powerful indictment and by and large Frost emerges from it as a
cunning, cold self-seeker, thoroughly prepared to lie, cheat and
wound in order to win yet another crumb of adulation. When he
had a new book coming out, he would deliberately set out to in-
gratiate himself with prospective reviewers or influential editors;
when prizes were in the offing he would make sure that he was on
good terms with the jury; when a rival poet seemed to be making

ground, he would attempt to impede his progress by private vili-
fication; when he scented the imminent power of a possibly hostile
critic, he would neutralize the threat by making friends with him.
All this, of course, was done in private; the public posture was of
lovable, plain-dealing self-reliance, and he was careful to avoid not
just criticizing his contemporaries (or praising them, come to that)
but also revealing too explicitly many of his unfashionable political
beliefs—he hated the thirties radicals but he had an opportunist's
nose for the coming orthodoxy.

These stratagems are untangled with care by Lawrance Thompson, but not just with care. There is more than an undercurrent of
malice also. Having made up his mind that Frost was a Machiavel-
lian, Thompson rarely finds it possible to give him the benefit of the
doubt; in other words, almost any friendly, decent gesture Frost
makes is attributed to manipulative skill rather than to friendship or
decency. Looking back to the first volume, where Thompson first
begins to develop his 'line' on Frost's careerism, we can see the
method at its most dubious. Announcing that Frost, after his arrival
in England, had consciously decided to embark on an 'almost desperate campaign of self-promotion', Thompson goes out of his way
to twist the evidence. Frost's relations with Pound are given as a
principal instance of ingratiation ('more pertinent to his immediate
campaign was the need for cultivating the attentions of Ezra
Pound'); but it took Frost a month to get round to answering
Pound's invitation to meet him and although Pound did write a
rave review of *A Boy's Will*, it was not to the author's liking and
Frost missed no chance thereafter to disparage his not unpowerful
'discoverer'. Similarly Frost didn't take to Yeats, refused to meet
Amy Lowell (although the first thing he was to read on returning to
America was a fulsome piece by her on *North of Boston*) and fell out
with F. S. Flint. Thompson concedes that the people Frost really
liked in England were Wilfrid Gibson, Ralph Hodgson and Edward
Thomas, but he none the less presents Frost's relations with Gibson
and Hodgson (he could hardly have questioned the genuineness of
the Frost–Thomas friendship) as subtly self-advancing. And so the

'case' is built. Indeed so zealously suspicious is the biographer that
he is able to invest the mere act of submitting work for publication
with a somehow disgraceful glow: 'In his persistent campaign on
behalf of his poetry, Robert Frost had begun correspondence with
more than one American publisher.'

With Frost back in America, Thompson employs a similar technique. When the poet's American publisher greets him warmly and
suggests that he should attend a Poetry Society meeting and have
lunch with an editor, Frost is seen as 'ready to participate in any
campaign strategies and tactics which might advance his reputation'.
When Frost sends copies of his books to an unsuccessful poet-friend
whom he had long ago fallen out with, the act is assumed by Thompson to have been 'vindictive'. The friend did not think so, and wrote
back in generous terms. Thompson's confident verdict: 'Such a
letter might have succeeded in making Frost regret and even relin-
quish his unforgiving attitude toward Carl, but it did not. Burell
received no answer.'

'There is no baser form of hypocrisy than a false air of disinterested-
ness,' wrote Frost, and certainly in his letters to trusted friends like
Louis Untermeyer he made no bones about the necessity for the
poet to manage his affairs as skilfully as he knew how: 'The time
draws near for going to press and I must get as many editors as
possible implicated in the book beforehand. Ain't I wily?' Unattrac-
tive, yes, but anyone who has done any editing knows that Frost's
tactics are not so peculiar as Thompson makes them sound; the un-
usualness is in hearing them voiced so brutally. And here again, one
has to qualify the biographer's suggestion that Frost's success was in
some important aspects fabricated; the fact is that most of his
favourable reviews, college appointments, reading assignments,
Pullitzer Prizes and the rest came to him out of the blue. Only a
handful of unimportant triumphs could be said to have actually been
rigged; and these were more than balanced by Frost's considerable
facility for making enemies. When it came to the point, Frost was
the reverse of ingratiating in his dealings with literary figures he had
no respect for: thus, although Thompson describes his motive for

visiting Witter Bynner as 'timorous', the evening ended with Bynner emptying his beer over Frost's sarcastic head.

All in all, then, although no amount of charity would have been able to present Frost as a specially likeable personality (the account also shows him withstanding dreadful personal setbacks with a strange combination of guilt, resilience and self-pity), there does seem to be in Thompson's treatment not a little of the vindictive impulse which he finds so repugnant in his subject. The next volume —the present one takes us up to the death of Frost's wife in 1938— will tell us how it came about that Thompson was appointed by Frost as his 'official' biographer. So far, although Thompson first met Frost in 1926 and was by 1936 disciple enough to organize a Frost exhibition at Wesleyan University, we have been told nothing of the beginnings of a friendship which was to last from 1939 until the poet's death in 1963—though not, apparently, thereafter.

1971

A Poetry Chronicle

GEORGE BARKER
Dreams of a Summer Night

There were signs in George Barker's last book, *The View from a Blind I*, that the long, hectic fever had passed and that he was at last settling down to an exhausted, mildly ironical middle age. Random flashes of the old extravagance were still in evidence and there was a routine sprinkling of puns, but none of all this seemed in earnest any more. Nor, though, did his new manner. Being loftily scornful about the Beats was not a role to wring much zest from this arch-prophet of the Dionysian, and the casual, chatty note did not come at all naturally. Attempts at faintly wearied sophistication just did not have that fractionally managed tact and poise which Auden, say, takes so marvellously in his stride, and the intended flow of easy conversation rarely got beyond the merely bare and prosy. Though the book as a whole was probably more consistently intelligible than any of his others it was also a good deal duller, and false to his real gifts.

Quite what these real gifts are is still something of a mystery, since his successes have all been momentary and of rather different kinds. It is clear, though, that they are most usually displayed when he is least self-consciously trying to be sensible. At his most shrieking and inane, Barker always seemed able to hit off something fine and surprising; one tended to stick with him through the hot growths of sex disgust and religious frenzy on the offchance of a happy accident. A fairly dutiful journey most of the time, it must be said, but now and then rewarded. The high-pitched, boasting monotone might suddenly falter into a specific nervous tenderness, or it might swell into a legitimate, earned grandeur. Out of his profusion of grotesque images there might be one that had real depth and resonance. His theory that, to get at the unknown, poetry *must* distort appearances, since what is unknown cannot by definition be bodied forth by what is known, was obviously suicidal—doomed to produce a language and a landscape that could take pride in flaunting their distance from the 'natural'—but it gave him the licence he appeared to need, licence to take off and see what happened. Barker's work is amazingly uneven, but it is hard not to see this unevenness as a necessary price for those few distinguished lines and stanzas that oblige us still to take him seriously.

His new book continues where *The View from a Blind I* left off. If anything, since its subject is one which in the past has fired Barker to his most remote rhetorical extremes, it is more determinedly withheld and clear-headed. The subject is death, both the poet's own anticipated death, the sense he has of being haunted all the time by dead experience and by the deaths of certain friends whose memories continue to inhabit him, 'those who sleep in a strange cloud beside us'. There are a number of elegies; one to Oscar Williams, formal, speculative, and rather willed in its affection (the ending, in which Barker hopes for Williams and his dead wife that the grave will 'hold you both closer and together keep you' is presumably not *meant* to be a jovial metaphysical quip); one to Eliot, very literary and jokey (though Barker says that Eliot 'loved bad jokes' this is not excuse enough for adding one of his *Waste Land* notes to his obituary —intended though the gesture is to be knowingly cordial); and one to Louis MacNeice—the best of the lot, this, a bit sad and awkward in its genuineness—which reveals that he has been forgiven for having a garage. John Minton and Robert Colquhoun get what little of the old forties fire and doom the book can boast.

Friends, scenes, situations from the past, these swarm into nearly every poem; isolated moments of response or commitment to the living are invariably blurred by some nagging ghost, some black, diffusing intimation. There is little panic, very little really personal recoil; an uneasy resignation, a tendency to morose speculation, an enervated clinging to the old muddle of classical and Christian imagery, but no final sense of a whole, functioning personality. When anything concretely his own gets into the poems, Barker retreats from it into the mythological, the vaguely symbolic or the abstract, or he just lets it leak away through one of his porous evocatives—dream, golden and holy are the favourites in this book. In one of the better poems, Part V of the long title sequence, there is a good instance of this; the poem opens with a picnic on a Welsh hill, with the poet eating an apple and looking out across the countryside below. There is some neat description and a pleasant sense of a moment lazily enjoyed. A cemetery is spotted, though, and instead of it merely taking its place as part of what is seen (and by doing so *suggest* the obvious) it is ponderously pounced on:

> '*These without wishes or friends*,' *I thought*, '*they have their*
> *future already*
> *Sleeping in that quiet valley where nothing unexpected can awake*
> *Them and of all this landscape they alone are not part since*
> *They cast no shadows, they have their homecoming and the*
> *golden silence they dream in*
> *Is spread by a holier sun, never, like ours, due to set.*'

The moment is not only destroyed but is made to seem set up. There is a certain sloppiness of feeling, a too facile *in memoriam* kind of sadness running somewhere underneath these lines, and it is typical of Barker's new manner. We know what he is talking about, most of the time, but we are no longer sure that he cares about it.

1966

ELIZABETH BISHOP
Selected Poems

Randall Jarrell once summarized Elizabeth Bishop's message to her readers as, quite simply, 'I have seen it.' In the best of her early work, at any rate, she seems to make no more weighty claim than that; she is the poet of pure description, gratuitously pleased with what she sees. She does not, like William Carlos Williams, pretend to be re-conquering a continent every time some interesting landscape attracts her eye. As American and imagistically exact as Williams, she is not at all polemical or primitive, and nor is she afraid to be clever. She pursues an intricately local accuracy, and is dashingly successful. Complex natural arrangements are recaptured shape by shape, with an assured, geometrical precision. Miss Bishop likes maps, likes making them—'mapped waters are more quiet than land is'—and there is a topographical serenity about her wildest landscapes; they are static, petrified by vocabulary, and they have as much power to surprise us as their confident spectator has elected to permit them.

And it is here that one's admiration for Miss Bishop's mastery begins to falter—it is, in the end, too absolute. The cool, assembling eye is not nature's servant but its tyrant, its complacent victor. She is prepared to grant that there is much 'untidy activity' in nature, but the whole effort of her early work is towards the neat, the clean-edged, the describable. Like the 'Monument' she celebrates in one of her best-known poems, her poetry is 'an artifact' that

> *holds together better*
> *than sea or cloud or sand could by itself*
> *much better than real sea or sand or cloud.*

This landscape-gardening tendency is more marked in Miss Bishop's earlier work, though, than in the poems reprinted here from *Questions of Travel* (1966). Her scenes now are much less coolly detailed, more nervously resonant, than before. The world is still easily tamed, in places, but is more generally resourceful, more mysterious. It is mainly that Miss Bishop herself seems to have moved much more openly to the centre of her poetry; the auto-cratic intelligence is less in evidence and one senses now a whole vulnerable personality at work in lines like:

> *The sea's off somewhere, doing nothing. Listen.*
> *An expelled breath. And faint, faint, faint*

L

> (*Or are you hearing things*) *the sandpipers'*
> *heart-broken cries.*

The sandpiper crops up in another poem and it is through the bird's eyes that Miss Bishop acknowledges that 'The world is a mist. The world is uniquely/minute and vast and clear.' Without in the least admiring these dead lines, one can yet note that they could hardly have appeared in Miss Bishop's earlier poems. The situations in *Questions of Travel* are more humanly alive, more moving than in either of Miss Bishop's previous books and there are rhythmic echoes and a general quality of tense nostalgia that suggest she has learned something from her admirer and avowed disciple, Robert Lowell.

1967

ROBERT CREELEY
Poems 1950–65

'How much I should like to please,' writes Robert Creeley, 'it is a constant concern'—and his is indeed an ingratiating talent, depending centrally on a halting, thinly wistful kind of self-exposure, on lovable mannerism rather than a style that has been deeply suffered for. In spite of the displayed modesty, the poignant mild-heartedness, the air of artless experimentation that have won Creeley his multitude of borrowers, he is in fact an unremittingly self-conscious writer, both in the blatant cuteness of his emotional content and in the technical procedures he has rather woodenly inherited from William Carlos Williams. The content one can either take or leave, depending how engaging one finds aphorisms like:

> *To be loved is half the battle*
> *I thought.*
> *To be*
> *Is to be better than is not.*

Most of Creeley's overtures, whether they are meant as wisdom, advice or confession, work at this level of abstraction; now and then he touches on something specific and there is a brief flicker:

> *When I know what people think of me*
> *I am plunged into my own loneliness. The grey*
> *hat bought earlier sickens.*

Even here, though, there is something too slickly assured in his sadness; he is not alone, one eye is on the audience.

A good deal of this measured, slightly preening, aspect of his delivery clearly derives from the kind of forms he deals in: the short, chopped-up line, the tricksy, double-talking line breaks, the shallowly contrived congruity between what is being said and the shape it is awarded, and so on. Creeley's idea, as it was Williams's, is to write a poetic language that is distinctively American. This is not, unfortunately, just a matter of the odd 'for Chrissake', nor is it anything drably phonetic—it is an effort that involves the total structure of each poem. As we all know, there is no such thing as an agreed American vernacular; a poet is stuck with his own set of cadences and the aim must be to get his struggle with them accurately simulated on the page. What the reader, or viewer, is finally supposed to experience is not just one man's idiom but a typographical representation of the physical labour (the breath, pulse-rate, etc.) that has gone into fashioning it. As with the charm, so with the cadence; if we are not tuned in, too bad—we will be left with something stuttering, short-winded, flat and, if he says so, thoroughly American.

1966

JOHN FULLER
The Tree That Walked

The wit and ingenuity that marked John Fuller's first collection, *Fairground Music*, owed more to Auden and to Wallace Stevens than to the ruling figures of the fifties; indeed, its gratuitous vitality served to mock the more drably moralizing aspects of the Movement and to insist that neat forms, intelligence and mannered diction need not necessarily involve a strangulated, dismally equivocating attitude to the emotions.

The Tree That Walked is every bit as elegant and resourceful as the earlier volume. There are poems in it which read like entries for some impossible competition ('An Exchange Between the Fingers and the Toes', for instance, and a salivating psalm on the delights of cooking) and there are some rather routine, speculative essays that are smooth and clever but too comfortably smiling. There are also some weirdly fertile, self-indulgent fantasies. But it is in the sequence of poems set in America and—even more strikingly—in the handful about suburban domesticity that Fuller is most impressive, more direct and resonant than before but no less poised. It is these, it seems to me, that mark the new book's real development.

The American poems are ironic snapshots; the continent is seen, self-mockingly, with a tourist's eye and there is no faked-up familiarity, no fashionable courting of apocalypse. The stance throughout is of repelled and detailed curiosity. Fuller is more impressive in his account of America's vulgar surfaces than in his slightly inert gestures towards what ungovernably lies beneath them, 'the furies' which the 'civic idea pacifies', but the total vision of a wild and secret continent which the shoddy artifices of technology can merely make a coarse pretence of having tamed is documented with a fine perceptiveness, a peaceable alarm.

The naturalistic vividness of these poems seems to have cleared the ground for what are finally the book's most arresting pieces; 'Green Fingers', 'Goodbye to the Garden' and 'The Pit' all in one way or another permit Fuller's personal furies to discard their haunting robes and visit him at home, in the silent, dreaming desperation of a suburbia whose quotidian detail he catches as expertly as ever but now convincingly infects with menace. Though he still turns over-eagerly from metaphor to discourse, it is significant that in these poems Fuller abandons rhyme and is altogether more relaxed in his delivery, more intimately self-expressive than he has tried to be before. Already the most intelligent poet of his genera-

tion, he now seems excitingly prepared to place less than a total faith
in pure intelligence:

> The nights come in slowly. Behind a half-curtain
> The impossible is completed. A single lamp
> Weighs down its ornaments in pools of light.
> Shadows crawl over the crater, roped
> To the terrain's recoil, roped to the pit.

1967

TED HUGHES
Crow

After *Lupercal*, Ted Hughes's bestiary seemed to be complete, and
there was much wondering at the time (though more in private than
in print) about where this gifted poet would go next. Beastless,
would Hughes allow the fevered, apocalyptic rhetoric that had been
ominously omnipresent in his first book, *A Hawk in the Rain*, to
reassert itself or would he try to develop the naïve, generalizing
commentaries on human conduct ('With man it is otherwise') that
were inserted here and there in *Lupercal*? The justified suspicion was
that in a period of tame, chatty, effortfully rationalistic verse, it was
rather easy to overrate a poet who possessed even the beginnings of
linguistic vigour; to mistake, in Hughes's case, a souped-up, rippl-
ingly muscular, neo-Georgianism for something much more wise
and novel than it really was.

At the same time, though, there was a general unwillingness
among critics and reviewers to blur the advent of 'a poet of the first
importance' (A. Alvarez) by making too much of such qualms; for
example, by examining too closely the considerable discrepancy
between the delicacy of Hughes's eye and the crudity of most of his
ideas—by pointing out, in short, that if this poet were to apply to
human beings even a fraction of the fond exactitude he brought to
bear on animal behaviour, he would not find it possible to deal, as in
Lupercal he almost exclusively did deal, in cartoons rather than in

characters (the pimply clerk, the Mafeking colonel, the prize village boozer, and so on); cartoons employed, moreover, to support a vague, simple-mindedly asserted preference for the primitive, the brutal and the sudden as against (need one bother to trot out the hoary antitheses?) the cerebral, the sophisticated, the hesitant.

The absence from Hughes's work of any complex or subtle human personality continued to be worrying throughout the ambiguously aimed *Earth-Owl and Other Moon-People* and the somewhat thrown-together package of stories, plays and verse entitled *Wodwo*. In both books, Hughes's gift for fierce and thrilling natural observation was intermittently in evidence, but so too were his most striking faults: the flailingly portentous verbiage, the indulged relish for the violent and the painful, the deep authorial evasiveness, the skimped and shallow dealings with the human world, and so on. The problem of not having any more animals to write about he sinisterly solved by, quite simply, inventing imaginary ones or (as with his jaguar) revamping an old favourite. The horrific nursery frieze assembled in *Earth-Owl* was not just a marginal departure. It was a sketch of things to come, and the bursts of Gothickry that kept cropping up in *Wodwo*, rather suggested that Hughes, far from looking for a way of directing his linguistic gifts back to the human world (where, admittedly, they would need to have been refined, made more tentative, less self-admiring), was indeed seeking an area in which those gifts could be exercised even more randomly than hitherto. He was seeking, in short, a territory and a device which would enable him to unload his obsessions without requiring that he test them out, in any precise way, against reality.

The device and territory of *Crow* are perfectly chosen for this purpose. Crow's naturalistic presence, so far as he has one, allows some scope for Hughes's old bestiarizing gifts; his theological presence— he is simultaneously God's partner, God's victim, God's godless Man —is vague and immense enough to permit unlimited portentousness; his human stance—tough, sardonic, blood-soaked—is so deliberately (and fashionably) cartoon-like for it to seem an irrelevance to complain of its utter superficiality.

The world that Crow moves in, is an emblem for, is drenched in blood, racked with agony, devastated by numerous varieties of violence. He views it with an eye proprietorial, laconically appalled yet also sadistically gratified. Standing for nothing, he can stand for anything, and moves effortlessly from God's right hand, through the Garden of Eden, to battlefields and blacknesses both old and new. The agent of evil or the principle of enduring, suffering humanity; the villain or the victim? Well, both, of course, for are they separable? Once this malleable symbolic function has been grasped, the reader can settle down to enjoy the creature's grisly travels; enjoy, indeed, a cosy, unperplexing wallow.

The majority of the poems in *Crow* are built on the catalogue, and sometimes the crescendo principle; the formula is simple and totally hospitable. Take a phrase like, for example: 'Black was the . . .' and invent resonant attachments to it. 'Black was the heart/Black the liver', 'Black the blood in its loud tunnel', 'Black the bowels packed in furnace/Black too the muscles'. When the animal anatomy is exhausted, move on to abundant Mother Nature: 'Black is the rock', 'Black is the otter's head'. Another method is the question and answer session, with either question or answer remaining constant throughout:

> *Who owns these scrawny little feet?*
>   Death
> *Who owns this bristly scorched-looking face?*
>   Death
> *Who owns these still-working lungs?*
>   Death
> *Who owns this utility coat of muscles?*
>   Death
> *Who owns these unspeakable guts?*
>   Death

or

> *Where is the Black Beast?*
> *Crow, like an owl, swivelled his head.*

> *Where is the Black Beast?*
> *Crow hid in its bed, to ambush it.*

Or, more sophisticated, there is the 'When the . . . then the . . .'
strategy:

> *When the owl sailed clear of tomorrow's conscience*
> *And the sparrow preened himself of yesterday's promises*
> *And the heron laboured clear of the Bessemer upglare*
> *And the bluetit zipped clear of lace panties*
> *And the woodpecker drummed clear of the rotovator and the*
> *rose-farm*
> *And the peewit tumbled clear of the laundromat*
>
> *When the bullfinch plumped in the apple bud*
> *And the goldfinch bulbed in the sun*
> *And the wryneck crooked in the moon*
> *And the dipper peered from the dewball.*
>
> *Crow spraddled head-down in the beach-garbage, guzzling*
> *a dropped ice-cream.*

What these techniques have in common is that they grant total
licence to the poet's freewheeling inventiveness; when he runs out of
ingredients, the cake is baked. It is true to say of Hughes's list-poems
in this book that each of them could be half-a-dozen lines shorter or
half-a-dozen lines longer without being seriously damaged or en-
hanced. The formula depends on a mechanical, drugging repetition,
and the last thing we are asked to do is respond to or examine the
relevance and accuracy of individual components. Similarly, we
need not look for any rhythmic subtlety, nor any pondered or
incisive line-breaks; the liturgical scaffolding takes care of all
that.

Just as we are not invited to make severe formal or rhythmic demands of these poems, similarly much of the actual language hardly
bears examination. By employing rigid structural formulas and by

making the most of Crow's own deflatingly ironic disposition (though how cumbersome so many of his ironies in fact are), Hughes manages to contain some of his rhetorical belligerence, but there can be no disguising the fact that the central energies of this book are, in their eager pursuit of blood and thunder, only minimally tempered by poetic caution—that caution which insists on trying to connect words to their full meanings. Take, as a sample of the book's bludgeoning behaviour, this (not exhaustive) list of blood-images and ask yourself if their progenitor need ever have seen anybody bleed; not, admittedly, a clinching test but one well worth applying to a work which has been credited with affording us *new* insights into our bloody selves: 'God bled, but with men's blood'; 'Blood blasts from the crown on his head in a column'; 'Blood was too like water'; 'Shock-severed eyes watched blood/ Squandering as from a drain-pipe/Into the blanks between stars'; 'Screaming for Blood'; 'All this messy blood'; 'Black is the gall lying on the bed of the blood'; 'As he drowned in his own blood'; 'Blood her breasts her palms her brow all wept blood'; 'He stands trousered in blood and log-splits/The lolling body, bifurcates it/Top to bottom, kicks away the entrails—/Steps out of the blood-wallow'; 'His wife and children lie in their blood'; 'The suddenly dropped, heavily dropped/Star of blood on the fat leaf'; 'Drinking Beowulf's blood, and wrapped in his hide'; 'Smiles that went off with a mouthful of blood'; 'The pavement and the air and the light/Confined all the jumping blood/No better than a paper bag.'

One could compile a similar, similarly oppressive and similarly undisturbing, list involving Death or Disease (facile play with 'tattered guts', 'shattered brains' and 'death's mouldy tits' abounds), and one could point also to the book's key violent-verbs—stabbing, smashing, screaming, writhing, and so on. The measure of the sensibility behind the words is to be discovered in the way most of these words are mechanically chucked in, lazily relished, insultingly (to actual suffering) exploited.

One of the most significant poems in *Crow* is called 'Lovesong'; the described lovers are vampiric, gluttonous, destructive, bent on a

brutal, absolute possession of each other. The significance of the
poem is not in the black view it takes of human love (though this, as
we have seen, is hardly insignificant) but in the way it (gluttonously,
vampirically) piles blackness upon blackness, the way it seems—after
the first dozen lines or so—to have moved far beyond any real
gravity or wisdom into a horror-comic realm of barely controllable
fascination with its own subject-matter. An important quality for
poets is knowing exactly where to stop; this poem, like so many
others in this brutal book, not only does not know, but does not
care. It flogs on until it is drained, replete.

1971

ELIZABETH JENNINGS
Collected Poems

Although Elizabeth Jennings was closely involved in all the Movement business of the early fifties (she was in *New Lines*, had a Fantasy
Press pamphlet, and so on) she was never a fully paid-up member of
that witty band; learned debunkery, William Empson, villanelles—
none of this had any charm for her. There was, after all, something
rather tweedily male about the whole Movement enterprise.

What clearly did engross her, though, was the prevailing view of
poetry as a handy instrument of the intelligence, a shapely, complicated vehicle for paradox and speculation, a means of being quietly
reasonable. Her early poems tended to be comfortably musing or
knowingly anecdotal, pursuing problems of philosophy and morals
with a contented bafflement, as if to pose them neatly were some
kind of improving substitute for the anguish that might be involved
in actually trying to solve them; she was sensible and symmetrical
and only now and then allowed experience to cloud her cool abstractions—as in 'Reminiscence', for example, where she admits to
having grown 'too subtle' and recalls a time when she could
respond directly to sensuous delights and be 'happy not to have it
clear'.

Her language, even in wistful poems of this sort, was drably un-assertive. One never felt that she was suppressing vital gifts. 'Emo-tion's not explained by thought alone', 'I have an aching thirst/That can't be quenched by a cool mind'. There was this constant under-tone of self-accusation but always too bland and enervated to threaten any interesting disruptions. The curious feature of Miss Jennings's subsequent development is that although she has become more and more preoccupied with irrational experience—religion, madness—and more prepared also to make use of material from her private life, she has not significantly outgrown the gentle, muting habits of her early work. She is aiming now, it seems, for a poetry that is direct and revelatory, that copes unflinchingly with—in parti-cular—the subject of mental breakdown. There is a kind of neu-tralizing discrepancy, though, between the manifestly dreadful situations she is concerned with and the sensible, appeasing style which is the only way she knows of giving voice to them.

Attempts for a more nervously expressive manner merely result in some unsuccessful free-association pieces, and there is clearly no point in urging her to be more violent or theatrical. As it is, there are certain poems, and in particular those about other people's suffering, which suggest that she might yet make moving poetry out of what now appears to be her work's most crippling disability —her refusal to surrender a reasonableness which she no longer has any real faith in.

1967

HUGH MACDIARMID
Collected Poems and *A Lap of Honour*

One of Hugh MacDiarmid's better known poems is called 'The Kind of Poetry I Want', and there is a sense in which his entire out-put might happily be gathered together under a single heading of this kind. He has always been a good deal more interested in pro-grammes than in poetry; indeed, his programmes have rarely given poetry much of a chance. He has, for instance, rejected what he calls 'The irresponsible lyricism in which sense impressions/Are employed to substitute ecstasy for information' and declared himself in favour of 'a poetry which fully understands that the era of technology is an established fact'.

Easy enough to fly flags, and of course 'lyricism' grows on trees, but what does such fiery sloganizing add up to on the page? Fans claim that MacDiarmid has triumphantly fashioned a loose, discursive, open-ended kind of meditative vehicle which is hospitable to ideas, facts and arguments, that he has marvellously broken free of fiddling post-symbolist constraints. The unconvinced complain that he has merely granted himself a licence to be boringly opinionated, that he has ditched rhythm, metaphor and formal discipline in order to make room for muddled, self-admiring chat.

The success of the kind of poetry MacDiarmid wants (if success can be envisaged for an aesthetic enterprise that trades in 'ecstasy' for 'information') finally depends on the quality of the intelligence it seeks to exhibit. We could maybe tolerate the prosy flatness of MacDiarmid's language, its poverty of imagery and verbal subtlety, we could even overlook the frequently intruded slabs of leaden Marxist theory, the geology and the philology, if we could locate at the centre of it all a mind of any real distinction. Here again, though, MacDiarmid is rather better at telling us what we need than he is at actually supplying it:

> Clear thought is the quintessence of human life.
> In the end its acid power will disintegrate
> All the force and flummery of current passions and pretences,
> Eat the life out of every false loyalty and craven creed
> And bite its way through to a world of light and truth.

It is this kind of banality that time and again brings MacDiarmid's theories down to earth, and confines him to the role of ardent pleader for objectives which he is manifestly unequipped to reach.

The same burden of self-consciousness sits on his much-praised dialect poems. Never quite so explicitly, or lengthily, programmatic as his later work, they rarely seem to cut free of their pedantic duty to the so-called Scots Renaissance. Scotland may well be grateful to MacDiarmid for his solemn, loyal efforts to rebuild its literary culture, but to the unkilted reader there is something quaint, and rather bogus, in the dredged-up archaisms of literary Lallans. Reading, for instance, of 'mither-fochin' scones' we turn with interest to the glossary only to find that 'to foch' in MacDiarmid's Scotland is 'to turn (used of scones on a griddle)'. If poetry cannot be wrung from the language Scotsmen speak, no amount of scholarly nostalgia is going to help.

The enlarging of the glossary, incidentally, is one of the few revisions that have now been made to MacDiarmid's 1962 *Collected Poems*; he has removed the notorious 'Perfect' (replacing it with a poem that is conveniently of the same length) and has acknowledged some other borrowings—these changes have been made on the strength of the hilarious *Times Literary Supplement* correspondence of two years ago in which line after line of MacDiarmid was revealed to have been written by someone else. The new book *A Lap of Honour* is not really new at all, but consists of poems which were omitted from the *Collected Poems*. MacDiarmid's note in the *Collected Poems* that it includes all the poems that he wishes to preserve was written before he knew that the *Lap of Honour* poems were to be omitted—this note, curiously enough, has not been removed from the new edition.

MacDiarmid is now seventy-five, and a *Lap of Honour* is as good a way as any of marking the occasion—more sensible, certainly, than the sycophantic verse-tributes that are collected in *Poems Addressed to Hugh MacDiarmid*. All the familiar faces of the Scots Renaissance beaming in unison, and a preface by Compton Mackenzie! Those Burns Nicht revellers whom MacDiarmid so despises may yet have the last laugh.

1967

W. D. SNODGRASS
After Experience

Eight years ago, W. D. Snodgrass published his first collection of poems, *Heart's Needle*. It was a strange book; very mannered and literary, brimming over with technique (Snodgrass had been a star student at Iowa's Poetry Workshop) and yet, in one fine poem—the long title sequence about the poet's separation, by divorce, from his young daughter—much more harrowingly intimate and impassioned than almost anything else that was appearing at the time. It was intimate in the manner of Lowell's *Life Studies*, which had appeared in the previous year; that is to say, there was a completely open, unembarrassed factuality in its treatment of personal experience. There were no masks, no modesties; the poet had become his own biographer.

Life Studies was the better book; it was more richly deliberate in its unburdenings, more historically resonant (Lowell had, of course, the luck to be a Lowell) and much more relevantly skilful. But the two poets had enough in common for a small movement to be foisted on them; that of 'confessional poetry', a genre which has since been discredited by sundry imitators. 'Confessional' was an unfortunate way of describing what was new about *Life Studies* and *Heart's Needle*—the term reeks of guilt and ingratiation—but it does recall the general surprise that such poetic vibrance and composure could be won from subjects that seemed doomed to privacy or narcissistic inflation.

There is nothing in Snodgrass's second book, *After Experience*, that is quite so arresting and memorable as *Heart's Needle*, and the tendency to over-elegance is now even more marked. This last, in particular, is a real disappointment because the fiddling neatness that marked so many of the poems in the first book could be indulged then as the consequence of too much homework at Iowa. Now it begins to look like an aspect of the poet's sensibility, and it doesn't help that Snodgrass feels content to mock it: 'Now I can earn a living/By turning out elegant strophes'.

In a poem called 'April Inventory' (in *Heart's Needle*) Snodgrass took a sad, mildly scoffing, look at his position as a university teacher; in his new book he smiles similarly at his position as a 'practising' professional poet: 'I must memorize you, bit by bit/ And must restore you in my verses/To sell to magazines'. He must have smiled, too, as he typed out the list of acknowledgments with which the book is prefaced; he is 'indebted to' the National Endowment in the Arts, the Corporation of Yaddo and the Macdowell Colony, he has composed Phi Beta Kappa ceremonial poems at Columbia University and at William and Mary College, he has had a grant from the National Institute of Arts and Letters, a fellowship in poetry from the *Hudson Review*, and—of course—the Pulitzer Prize.

The list is depressing not because Snodgrass has had more of this kind of patronage than his colleagues (though he probably has) but because there is in the book precisely the tailored competence, the empty, stylish craftsmanship that one might gloomily anticipate from the endowed professional. Whether the prizes produce the polish or vice versa it is impossible to say, but it is not easy, faced with verse so well written and worked up as this, to separate them altogether.

There would be no point in grumbling, of course, if Snodgrass did not seem still to be capable of real excellence. In the dozen or so poems that open the book, the old power to stab at the right detail, to talk in a voice that is at once poised and inflamed, to flood the whole poem with a sense of gentle pleading and unbearable regret— all this is still there. In these poems he runs close, as many of the best poets do, to sentimentality, to pushing so far into areas of tenderness and fragility that it seems impossible that he won't slop over into something false—indeed now and then he does just that—or that he won't pull up short and act tough. In poems like 'September', 'The First Leaf', 'Takeoff', in parts of 'Leaving Ithaca', and in some of his translations Snodgrass brings it off.

1968